A Bucket Full Of Miracles

Preaching The Miracles Of Jesus

Cycle A

Jeff Wedge

CSS Publishing Company, Inc., Lima, Ohio

A BUCKET FULL OF MIRACLES

Library of Congress Cataloging-in-Publication Data

Wedge, Jeff.
   A bucket full of miracles : preaching the miracles of Jesus : cycle A / Jeff Wedge.
      p. cm.
   ISBN 0-7880-2318-7 (perfect bound : alk. paper)
      1. Jesus Christ—Miracles—Sermons—Outlines, syllabi, etc. 2. Lectionary preach-
ing. I. Title.
BT366.3.W43 2004
251'.6—dc22   2004010409

For more information about CSS Publishing Company resources, visit our website at
www.csspub.com or e-mail us at custserv@csspub.com or call (800) 241-4056.

ISBN 0-7880-2318-7   PRINTED IN U.S.A.

Dedicated to
the Pastor and People of
Hope Lutheran Church,
Daytona Beach, Florida,
where miracles still happen.

Table Of Contents

Introduction

The church I attend has a technique for introducing the children's sermon which was new to me when I joined the congregation. Each week someone, usually one of the children but sometimes an adult, is given a bucket, and asked to place something in it which will be used as the basis for next week's children's sermon.

One week, a woman in the congregation had prepared the children's sermon. She sat on the floor with the children and began by asking them what they thought a miracle was. Then she pointed out that the gospel had been a story about a miracle, and she told them she had a bucket full of miracles for them. The entire congregation leaned forward slightly, to better see what in the world a bucket full of miracles might look like.

Most people would lean forward at least a little to see what the bucket might contain. It is a cliché these days, to point to the way we have become a little jaded, full of everything we have seen and heard, and finding it difficult to be really amazed by anything we encounter. This is a problem we might classify as a loss of wonder. Even the miracles in the Bible, particularly the miracles of the gospels, are so familiar we often have difficulty mustering any sense of wonder at them. Now they are more likely to be greeted with a bored yawn than with a sense of excitement and wonder.

Another problem is the modern world we find ourselves in. We are surrounded by things that would have been regarded as miracles in many past generations. Today things that are regarded as commonplace were previously thought to be impossible or even inconceivable.

Consider my eyes. I can now, literally, see better than I could for many years. This is largely a matter of the two cataract operations I have had. History says Jefferson Davis by the end of the Civil War was almost blinded by cataracts. So was I, once upon a time. Two painless, unreasonably simple (at least from my perspective) operations later, and I now see better than I have since I was in fourth grade, when I started to wear glasses.

Have I been the recipient of a miracle? For much of history, it would certainly have been so regarded. Today, it is a very common experience, as I rediscover every time I mention I've had a cataract operation. So, it seems, has almost everybody else, or at least a large number of people in my age group. Those who haven't yet had the operation seem to either know at least a few people who have had it or they are preparing for their own operation in the near future.

Perhaps another example might be in order. I have also had a stroke, a very mild one, which resulted in double vision for a time after the stroke. The doctors assured me such a problem was minor, and usually cleared up eventually. It was bothersome, and necessitated closing one eye to see relatively clearly, and it meant I couldn't drive. One Sunday, during worship, my vision cleared up. Was it a miracle? Or was it merely a coincidence?

For many years scholars spent much of their time in the effort to explain the miracles in terms of the natural world, without any intrusion into what we see around us every day from any outside source. Today, technology and imagined technology have combined to render many things less wondrous than they used to seem. Both because of the way things work and the ways things are thought to work (in the movies and on television, largely), it can be difficult to identify a miracle with any certainty. Things are even more difficult when divine intervention is expected to be involved. There are so many things that technology has brought us that it can be difficult to wonder at anything.

Does any of this mean the miracles didn't happen? Not at all, the problem is that in an age when the mechanisms of how things work are so important, the mechanics of the miracles are usually not all that important. Miracles are simply miraculous, what is most important is what comes to us when we hear about them — a sense of wonder and awe at the events recorded.

Rachael Carson once wrote a book titled *The Sense Of Wonder*. It is about some walks she took with her grand-nephew, at different times, and his excitement and wonder at the discovery of the natural world. She writes, "If a child is to keep alive his sense of wonder ... he needs the companionship of at least one adult who can share it, rediscovering with him the joy, excitement and mystery of the world we live in" (p. 45).

We all need to recapture something of that sense of wonder in order to understand the stories of the miracles properly, for underlying all the miracles is that sense of and contact with the joy, excitement, and mystery of the world we live in. Without that sense of wonder, the miracles are impossible to understand.

Miracle One

Nativity

The Text

Now the birth of Jesus the Messiah took place in this way. When his mother Mary had been engaged to Joseph, but before they lived together, she was found to be with child from the Holy Spirit. Her husband Joseph, being a righteous man and unwilling to expose her to public disgrace, planned to dismiss her quietly. But just when he has resolved to do this, an angel of the Lord appeared to him in a dream and said, "Joseph, son of David, do not be afraid to take Mary as your wife, for the child conceived in her is from the Holy Spirit. She will bear a son, and you are to name him Jesus, for he will save his people from their sins." All this took place to fulfill what had been spoken by the Lord through the prophet: "Look, the virgin shall conceive and bear a son, and they shall name him Emmanuel" which means "God is with us." When Joseph awoke from sleep, he did as the angel of the Lord commanded him; he took her as his wife, but had no marital relations with her until she had borne a son; and he named him Jesus.

This first miracle of the year is one which is fraught with dangers for a preacher.

First, there is the day when it appears in the calendar — the Fourth Sunday Of Advent. The entire Advent season is difficult at best. Precisely what the entire season is about is not always easy to hold in mind. If it is a time to prepare for the coming of Christmas,

11

this lesson seems to represent a serious instance of "Christmas creep."

The lessons for the first three Sundays of this year are all eschatological in nature, even the middle two which encapsulate the story of John the Baptizer. These earlier lessons remind us of the historical theme of Advent as a season focusing on the end of things, not the beginning. But this lesson is different.

Second, if the season presents difficulties, the lesson itself is, for all its familiarity, potentially difficult as well. The text preceding this is problematic for us, as well as almost invisible. This text contains difficulties in both the attitude of Joseph, the translation and use of Isaiah's prophecy, and the fulfillment of the prophecy which concludes the lesson.

Finally, this Sunday has often become a day in the contemporary church for a shortened or omitted sermon in light of the annual Christmas pageant or the special music which is traditionally offered this day. And, of course, Christmas carols are often added to the worship on this day with the excuse that this allows the singing of the old favorites without the time constraints of a very brief Christmas season.

Remarkably, in the face of all these difficulties, the Matthean account of the birth of Jesus does present a fertile source of preaching possibilities. It is well worth struggling with the difficulties to bring forth the message of this lesson.

About The Text

For many people the New Testament begins with a boring thud. The first sixteen verses of the volume, after all, are long lists of people who are mostly unknown, with names difficult, if not impossible to pronounce. Then there is a summary of what has just been detailed.

Only after this less than scintillating beginning, do we finally get to something like the story of Jesus. Matthew's genealogy, a text only rarely considered as suitable for reading during worship, much less as a basis for a sermon, is certainly a poorly regarded

12

opening for the larger story. Luke also has a genealogy, but he at least hides it further into the gospel. This Matthean opening is an almost invisible portion of the gospel. Obviously it was important to Matthew, especially since it is the first thing he mentions, but it has little meaning for most people today.

Our lesson begins by connecting to verse 16 and verse 17. In the first few words Matthew repeats both the idea of the birth of Jesus from 16 and establishes the identity of Jesus as the Messiah (from v. 17). Clearly Matthew has begun with a magisterial list establishing Jesus' Davidic lineage, and is now shifting to the more specific focus on the life of Jesus which will inform the remainder of what he writes.

Words

Jesus the Messiah — Verse 1:18 begins with a textual difficulty, one which is difficult for even those who are experts in textual criticism. The problem is easily seen in comparing the text of the NRSV, which is used here, and that of the RSV, which read "Jesus Christ." To make things even more difficult, some ancient manuscripts also read either "Jesus" or "Christ," but don't include both terms. The result is a series of questions that calls all the readings into a certain amount of doubt.

Jesus, by itself, is certainly appropriate here, but is it more of a reflection of the command of the angel in verse 21 than an original reading? The mere presence of the name is sometimes open to question, largely because of the presence of the definite article in the Greek.

Christ (either as a stand alone term, or as "the Christ," more a title than a name) appears quite appropriate and logically presents the most original sounding reading, but is the use actually an echo of the previous verse?

Jesus the Christ (or Messiah) is the reading found in the largest number of manuscripts, but as an expression which is extremely rare among New Testament manuscripts, is it a reading that would be used here virtually in isolation? Not only is the relative position of the elements ("Jesus" and "Christ") reversed in some manuscripts, the presence of the definite article, which is clearly found in the Greek, is a significant problem to a precise, unimpeachable understanding here.

Jesus Christ is the reading that seems to reflect the usage of the early church, but is it actually the earliest text?

And then we have the problem of translation. There are many people who firmly seem to believe that "Christ" is the family name of Jesus. The NRSV translation, at the least, works to correct this misunderstanding, while also preserving the connections between this phrase and verses 16, 17, and 21. In this place, it is likely that the title "Christ" is best understood by its translation, "the Messiah."

took place in this way — This lesson treads very carefully between the physical specifics of the situation and more general considerations, and this is the first phrase which treads the line. Clearly, the details of the process of birth are not the subject of these verses. In fact, Mary, and her participation in the events here is not a subject Matthew finds particularly attractive for exposition. The phrase is rather a way to introduce the broader context in which these events took place in a general, non-biological way.

she was found to be with child — In Greek the verb translated here is a passive form. Some translations make the action more active, with Mary discovering she is pregnant. The Greek form allows for less participation by Mary, since she is only found to be pregnant.

In reality, for Matthew this is a very impersonal discovery, with no indication of who found out, or how the details came to light. While it might be attractive to imagine a busybody, a gossip in the town, and all the attendant details, none of them are either stated or implied by the text.

Joseph, a righteous man — The word used to describe Joseph is another word that can cause problems in an interpretation of this text. "Righteous" is a term that can be understood in at least two ways. As a legal concept, it would refer to someone who was law-abiding, just, honest, and obedient. As a description of character, it would refer to someone who is good, compassionate, and kind.

14

The term is a favorite word of Matthew's, appearing more in this gospel than in the other three combined (nineteen times here, versus twice in Mark, eleven times in Luke, and three times in John). Usually Matthew seems to use the term to describe a person's character. But here, largely because of the reference to the legal term divorce, it is most often assumed to be used in a legal sense.

To some extent, it is Joseph's personality and the marriage customs of the time which are in question here. If we take Joseph as a kind, compassionate man, he can be seen as someone who had no desire to cause any more problems than he had to for Mary. Marriage customs of the day involved a process that took a period of time. Unlike the traditional customs most familiar today, it seems that the state of being married actually commenced (at least legally) before the couple began to cohabit. The relationship of Joseph and Mary had reached a point where they were considered to be married, even if neither physically intimate or cohabitating. Even without physical intimacy, it is probable that Joseph had a developing sense of affection for Mary, and his actions can easily be understood as a kindly attempt to end the relationship which he was no longer willing to share.

On the face of it, when Mary was found to be pregnant, the only explanation was that she was an adulteress. As such she was liable for the Old Testament punishment of stoning, although lesser punishments were likely more often available. Joseph, as a legalist, decides to terminate the marriage without demanding Mary's death. He feels, legally, that he is absolved of any responsibility for Mary since the child is obviously not his and he has a legal right to the expectation that his betrothed will be a virgin.

It is possible to insist that Joseph must be either a legalist or a compassionate man, but it is likely that he could have both feelings at the same time. Many other languages have less trouble expressing these two perspectives than English does. This is frequently accomplished by using a word signifying "correctness of action," which incorporates both compassion and legal correctness.

and — The Greek word here is *kai*, the most common word in the Greek text of the New Testament. It is also a word many people remember from a long-ago Greek class, because it most often is translated as "and." Ironically, the word is often not translated, particularly when it begins a sentence and serves more as a sort of punctuation than as a word conveying significant meaning.

The question here is how to translate the word. It might mean "but," quite as easily as "and" in this context. The resolution of this question depends on the way "righteous man" is understood. If it is taken in a legal sense, then a contrast would seem to be required here — the translation should be "but." If it is taken to signify a compassionate reaction to the situation — the translation need not indicate a contrast and should be "and."

Thus, the translation of this simple, common little word is the indicator of how "righteous man" is understood by the translator.

do not be afraid — This phrase seems to occur rather consistently when people in the New Testament are confronted with angels. Contrary to the modern view of angels as warm, comforting beings, in the Bible the initial reaction to their appearance, even in a dream, is an immediate, almost overwhelming fear. And this phrase, or some variation of it, seems to be the formula by which the angels begin to announce their messages.

Here the phrase seems to apply both to Joseph's reaction to the angel and his reaction to discovering that Mary is pregnant. In one case, it is a natural introduction to the action Joseph should be taking. In the other, it is a way to dispel Joseph's reluctance to proceed with his marriage plans.

to take Mary as your wife — Marriage customs at the time involved very little regard for "romantic love" as a reason for marriage. Rather, the steps involved in a marriage had implications beyond mere romantic attachment.

Many, if not most, marriages were arranged, often for purposes such as maintaining a family line (for example, a priestly family would, of necessity, marry another priestly descendant), establishing (or strengthening) a relationship between two families, or to conserve an inheritance (by marrying a relation). The actual marriage seems to have taken place in two stages, both of which were

16

likely accompanied by negotiations. The negotiations were likely more intense and drawn out in the first stage.

As a result of the first stage, not only did the husband and wife formally exchange consent before witnesses but the marriage contract was also agreed to. The marriage contract typically established the financial details about the upcoming marriage. It established both the marriage portion, the goods and money that remained the property of the wife, but which the husband controlled; and the dowery, the goods and money that became the property of the husband at the time of the marriage. Also possible was "marriage money" which the prospective husband paid to the bride's father to "purchase" the woman. If it seems that the woman had much in common with slaves, it should be noted that in the *Midrash* a query asking for any differences between acquiring a slave and acquiring a wife is answered in the negative.

After this first stage was completed, the couple were, in legal fact, married, even if they did not cohabit until the second stage. The husband had some rights over the person and property of his wife, and any sexual activity on the part of the wife could be construed as adultery. Further, a woman in this stage could be widowed or divorced, and there were cases of each. During this stage, the wife remained resident in her father's (or guardian's) house.

This first stage usually took place around the time the woman reached the age of twelve or twelve and a half. Until she was twelve, nothing a woman did (at least in relation to marriage) was considered valid, and could be dissolved at the father's whim. After twelve and a half, the woman was allowed to refuse to marry if she chose.

Approximately a year after the formal agreements were entered into, the second and final stage began. The most notable action here was the movement of the woman into the man's home, and the man's assumption of all responsibility for the woman's upkeep. Most often, this was also the point at which sexual relations would begin, although there is some evidence that certain areas allowed for rather limited contact during the first stage. Matthew's text makes it clear that such contacts were not part of his experience.

17

The angel is here telling Joseph to take Mary as his wife, that is, to enter into the second stage of the marriage procedure with her. Rather than divorcing Mary quietly, which was Joseph's first intention, the angel instructs Joseph to proceed with the second stage. It should be clear that Matthew seems to accept the idea that Joseph and Mary were already "married" in virtually every way but physically at this point.

to fulfill — This is the first use of the formula which is distinctive in this gospel. Matthew uses the formula for fulfilling the Old Testament prophecies at least ten times, possibly as often as fourteen times. In comparison, Mark's uses of a similar formula (four instances) are considered somewhat dubious as examples of a formulaic construction; while Luke has only one citation which is clearly a formula, and as many as five which was doubtful.

Matthew uses this formula to introduce citations from the Septuagint, but none of the citations are exact quotations. It might be that Matthew did not have the texts in front of him as he wrote, perhaps he had a defective set of citations, or perhaps he was quoting from memory. It is also possible that he made what he regarded as mild editorial corrections to the text to make the prophecies he is citing more applicable to Jesus and his situation. We simply do not know why the quotations are not exact. The fact that they are not exact seems to say something very important about Matthew's view of the unimportance of a verbal inerrancy of the text he was citing.

The quotation here is from Isaiah 7:14, where the most controversial word in the lesson — *virgin* — is the Hebrew generally taken to mean "young woman." Matthew, and the Greek word he uses clearly means a young woman who has not had sexual relations — a virgin. Matthew is making the events of Jesus' birth quite unique.

Emmanuel — The name to be applied to the child in Isaiah is Emmanuel. Thus, it is somewhat ironic that two verses later the child is actually named Jesus not Emmanuel. While the name Jesus is the name commanded by the angel, it is not the name to be expected as the fulfillment of Isaiah's prophecy. While this point is

18

often ignored, it is actually a prophecy which is fulfilled in this gospel.

In the last verse of the gospel (Matthew 28:20b) Jesus says, "And remember, I am with you always, to the end of the age." While the point is not particularly clear in translation, in the original Greek, the fulfillment becomes obvious. The answer given Moses, when he asked the burning bush for the name of God, is, in the Septuagint, "I am," or *Ego emi*. This phrase is often taken as a technical term for the name of God, as that is what appears in the text of Exodus 3:14, which established the name of God in response to Moses' inquiry.

The words of Jesus at the conclusion of the gospel are "*Ego* with you *emi*." More than merely a presence alongside, the Greek construction places the "with you" inside the name of God. Not merely is God with us, but we are enfolded within the Divine. This, finally, is the fulfillment of the promise of Emmanuel.

no marital relations with — When he concluded the second stage of the marriage process, Joseph had a legal right to sexual intercourse with his wife. In fact, there were customs and rules stipulating the expected frequency of such actions, which depended on the husband's occupation and the wife's condition (not pregnant, not menstruating, healthy, and so on). Joseph refrained from exercising his rights, apparently to ensure there would be no question of the parentage of the child, namely the son of Mary and the Holy Spirit.

This detail is, like many others in this lesson, seemingly a reflection of the physical contact, or lack thereof, involved in the process. Matthew, however, presents these details for a theological reason, to emphasize the unique nature of the birth of Jesus, not to satisfy any prurient interest or to titillate his readers. Most of the references are not precisely stated, and probably best avoided from the pulpit, even though they are certainly interesting and possibly suitable for a Bible study session.

The text makes it clear that Matthew is only interested in relations between Mary and Joseph prior to the birth of Jesus. There is no scriptural evidence here for the tradition of a stroke, or any other disability to Joseph immediately after the birth of Jesus, as is sometimes posited by traditions. In other words, sexual relations between Joseph and Mary are, without evidence to the contrary, quite likely as the normal course of events in a marriage after the birth of Jesus and the ritual cleansing of Mary.

Brothers of Jesus are mentioned in Mark 3:31 (and the parallels in Matthew 12:46 and Luke 8:19), 6:3 (and the parallel in Matthew 1:53-54, both of which also mention unnamed sisters), John 2:12 and 7:1-9. A variety of explanations have been offered for these relatives, such as the suggestion that the siblings were really step-siblings, or in some other way not the biological children of Mary. Such efforts depend entirely on extra-biblical material, traditions, suppositions, and often on theological desires. The entire question dates from a period after the New Testament was composed, and is not reflected in it at any point.

Parallels

The impact of the Christmas season notwithstanding, the biblical evidence concerning the birth of Jesus is actually quite slim. John has a philosophical prologue, which speaks of the birth only in John 1:14, that wonderfully carnal comment that "the Word became flesh and lived among us." But John offers no details about either the events or the process that brought this event to pass.

Mark is even less forthcoming. His Gospel begins with the commencement of the public ministry of an adult Jesus. He seems content to assume that the birth happened in the manner which might be expected for anyone.

The only other account we have of the birth of Jesus is in Luke. Comparing the accounts in Matthew and Luke leads to either confusion or a strong desire to conflate the two accounts. There are some basic agreements, with Matthew's agreement centered largely in these verses. When listed, these agreements seem to confirm some basic points of the stories, but they also leave large areas of disagreement and differing actions.

Joseph and Mary, the infant's parents, are legally engaged but not living together when the story begins. Joseph, who is of Davidic descent, is the subject of the angelic announcement of the coming birth (Mary is the subject in Luke's version). The conception is a result of the action of the Holy Spirit, not Joseph. The angel indicates the child will be the savior, and that his name should be Jesus. After the parents have begun living together, the child is born in Bethlehem, during the reign of Herod the Great, but is reared in Nazareth.

These are the points of agreement between the accounts of Matthew and Luke. Taken apart from any other details, they present a rather bland picture, hardly the full story found in either Matthew or Luke we are used to hearing at Christmas. But once we stray from these basic agreements, the disparities become quite large. Even in the listing of the points of agreement include a difference between the accounts, namely the individual who is the subject of the angelic visitation. In Matthew, the angel comes to Joseph in a dream. In Luke, we have the scene of the Annunciation to Mary. The differing focus of the two accounts leads to an introduction to the people of the story.

The People

As Individuals

As is often the case with incidents from the Bible, there is only one character in the story that is really presented in any depth. Ironically, in this lesson this individual is Joseph, and the text is the clearest picture we find of the man in the New Testament. There is not much detail here, and beyond this there are only a few passing references to the man.

Joseph is often presented as a carpenter, but the word in Greek often has a more general meaning of "one who builds or constructs, a craftsman." It has been pointed out that the term could be applied more specifically to makers of plows, or plows and yokes. The word appears only twice in the New Testament, in Mark 6:3, where it is applied to Jesus, and the parallel in Matthew 13:55, where it applies to Joseph.

It is possible that the fact of the same word being applied to the two men in a very similar context is a reflection of the tendency for

21

occupations to be passed from father to son. It could be merely an editorial change made by Matthew.

The reference in Matthew 13 is also significant for establishing the fact that Joseph seems to have been alive when Jesus began his public ministry. It seems likely that Joseph had died prior to the crucifixion, in light of Jesus' directions to the Beloved Disciple from the cross to care for Mary as her son (John 19:25b-27).

This is, to some extent, in conflict with the later traditions regarding Joseph's age. In the second century the idea that Joseph was an old man when these events took place was suggested by a pseudepigraphal gospel. In the fifth century it was first written that Joseph was 89 when he was widowed (and Jesus' step-siblings were all the result of this marriage), and 91 when Mary became his ward. But this chronology would mean Joseph would be over 120 when Jesus began his public ministry, a rather dubious claim.

While it was not uncommon for a husband to be older than his wife at that time (and throughout much of history, for that matter, down to the present day), there is no biblical evidence for an extreme age on the part of Joseph.

What we do have in this lesson is a picture of a man who finds himself in a difficult situation. His wife, at least in name, is pregnant and he is not the father since he has never known her sexually. If he divorces her publicly, she might be liable for the extreme punishment of stoning. It seems likely that during the months of negotiation to arrange the marriage, and during the first stage of the marriage, before cohabitation began, Joseph found he had some warm feelings for Mary. Even though he could not convince himself to go through with the second stage of the marriage in light of the clear evidence of Mary's misbehavior, he felt sympathetic enough toward her to be willing to handle things quietly. Certainly Mary was not the only instance of such a problem, and ways to dissolve a marriage contract informally had certainly grown up in the villages.

Perhaps there was a segment of the population that held stricter views of things than Joseph, and he feared that Mary might be attacked if the situation became known. There were certainly Essenes at the time, and they held a very strict interpretation of the

Law. Or there might have been other groups who held similarly strict views. It is possible that in Joseph's hometown such a group had gotten large enough to be a force in civic life.

Having reached a decision to resolve the situation in a discreet manner, Joseph had a dream. An angel in his dream told him to change his decision and continue with the marriage agreement. When the child was born, that Joseph was to name him Jesus. Joseph woke up with a resolve to follow the instruction of the angel, which he did. The picture that emerges here is of a man who was doing his best to follow the Law, but who was willing to temper the strictest tenets of the Law with a compassionate interpretation.

Of course, there is also the less attractive side of Joseph's character. He did, after all, decide to discard Mary for her apparent indiscretion. His kindness and compassion did not extend to consideration of the eventual results when Mary's actions would become known, as they certainly would. Even a quiet divorce required the husband to read the decree of divorce before two witnesses. And eventually, it would become known that Mary, an unmarried woman, had given birth to an illegitimate child. It is certainly possible to understand the account as presenting Joseph's compassion as originating in his own selfishness and desire for convenience.

As Images And Signs

Joseph is commemorated on March nineteenth as "the Guardian of our Lord," and this is the role for which he is most known. Both Matthew and Luke are careful, in their genealogies, to ensure Joseph is not thought of as the biological father of Jesus, but only as his father in a legal sense, or as the guardian of Jesus. Luke allows for the usage of calling Mary and Joseph "his parents" in the only story of Jesus between the infancy narratives and the beginning of his public ministry (Luke 2:41-51). Matthew is more restrained in his use of terms, consistently using the term "the child and his mother" to refer to Jesus and Mary.

Joseph is a symbol of parents and guardians who provide a loving, protective environment for the children entrusted to their care. The image he evokes is that of a faithful person who does the best he can to fulfill his duty. It is perhaps significant that much of what can be reconstructed of his life story must be done on the basis of inferences and suppositions. Often the people who devote themselves to the care and nurture of children are ignored in the larger picture of events. Mother's Day and Father's Day hardly begin to compensate for the historical lack of recognition. The image of Joseph as the guardian of Jesus is a strong reminder of the faithful service provided by those who follow in his path.

The Action

In The Story

In the account of the infancy of Jesus in Matthew, the will of God is made known through four dreams. Three of the dreams are Joseph's and are recounted in detail, one is reported without details as occurring to the Wise Men. All four dreams direct the actions of the participants in accordance with the divine plan and there is no demur to anything mentioned in a dream. The three dreams of Joseph all command actions leading to the fulfillment of prophecies.

Somehow, it is not difficult to accept people in the Bible who respond to commands given them by figures in dreams. They are accepted as one way God communicates with the people in the Bible. In the case of Matthew, at least in the stories he tells related to the birth and early years of the life of Jesus, dreams are a favored way for God to communicate with people. Even here, it is not God speaking directly, as is the case with Peter hearing a voice in a vision in Acts 10 and 11. In Matthew, the directions are given by angels. It shouldn't be forgotten that angels are messengers for God. They do not speak on their own, but only to convey God's commands to those who hear them.

One further aspect of Joseph's description as a "righteous man" is his obedience to the commands delivered to him by the angels of his dreams. Obedience to God's commands is an important aspect of righteousness, one which is sometimes overlooked. Acting as a righteous person is not simply a matter of following particular rules

24

established long ago. Jesus later makes this quite clear in this gospel, for example in Matthew 23. It involves both a matter of the heart (and the new rules written on the heart as described in Jeremiah 31.31-34) and obedience to specific directions given by such means as angels in dreams.

In The Hearers

To those who heard this story when Matthew's Gospel was assembled, it is likely that Joseph's behavior caused some comment. First, since Joseph is described as a righteous man, his behavior in actually marrying a woman who was obviously (seemingly) a sinner would be one source of surprise. Alternatively, a righteous man who was planning to act in an unrighteous manner by divorcing Mary, actually by not completing the marriage contract he had entered into, could also be a cause of surprise. The biggest surprise might be that it was a person of such obvious human frailty who was selected to be the guardian of Jesus.

Today, when we hear this story, it is easy to accept people who base their actions on dreams since those people are found in the Bible. When someone today says they are basing their actions on instructions they receive in dreams, many (if not most) people have serious doubts about the judgment, not to mention the sanity, of the person and the value of the actions based on the dreams.

Consider the scripts which sometimes appear in situation comedies. One of the people has a dream involving some reprehensible conduct by another character (the wife dreams that the husband leered at another woman, for example; or the husband dreams the wife went on a date with another man), and upon awakening, accuses the other character of wanting to behave in such a manner. While the scripts are often not the strongest of the season, they do point out the modern attitude. People who think dreams are real are funny, and when they act on the basis of dreams, they are even funnier.

This brings up another issue related to this story. Prophecies, and actions taken to fulfill prophecies, are acceptable in speaking of the past, but when people in the present speak of prophecies being fulfilled today, things are much more problematic. The first issue is the source of the prophecies, and then the attendant problem of prophetic understanding and interpretation. All too often, modern prophetic understandings seem entirely too close to fortune telling and quite removed from the tendency of the biblical prophets to level critiques against the society of their day for social injustices and unfaithful conditions among the people.

The Sermon

Illustrations

How can we understand the awe and mystery of the miracle of the incarnation?

A young boy asked his mother, "Is it true Jesus is everywhere?"

"Yes," mother answered, "Jesus is everywhere."

The boy then returned to staring out the window of the house. After a time looking out the window, he asked, without turning away, "Even in our backyard?"

Christmas preparations include finding just the right gifts.

A department store Santa was checking on a young man's Christmas spirit. "Have you gotten your sister a Christmas present, yet?"

"No," came the answer, "not yet."

"Are you going to get her something special? Even better than you got her last year?"

"That's going to be hard. Last year I gave her the measles."

Finding gifts can be a daunting experience for both the sales people and customers.

A frazzled salesman was trying to ring up a purchase for a customer, but the clamor of a busy season was distracting both of them. When the salesman asked if the customer wanted the purchase delivered, the customer seemed very relieved and agreed to the service. Then the salesman asked for the address. As he was entering the address in the proper place on the sales receipt, he commented, "It's a madhouse, isn't it?"

"No," replied the customer in an aggrieved tone, "it's a private residence."

A customer in a toy store asked a clerk about a toy. He responded, "That, ma'am, is an educational toy of the first magnitude. It prepares any child for adult life. No matter how the child puts it together, it's wrong."

Approaches To Preaching

To approach this as a pure miracle story would mean to emphasize the miracle of the incarnation. It is ironic that a lesson which avoids most discussion of the physical details of the story, even while it seems to discuss them quite frankly, tells of a miracle being described which is so completely physical. The very name of the miracle is a description of how physical it is. Incarnation comes from the Latin word *caro*, a noun meaning *flesh*. While the simple understanding is "in the flesh," it is easy to forget that Christianity, particularly at this point in the year, has a very physical emphasis. The Greek behind the Latin is *sarks*, a word defined as "material covering human or animal skeleton, *flesh*."

The miracle of the incarnation is one which places an emphasis on the actual, physical nature of the human body inhabited by Jesus. While it might be preferable to conceive of the body of Jesus as some sort of a special thing, not really afflicted by the same things that happen to everybody, it is a view that is contrary to the very word used to describe the miracle. Understanding and explicating the courage of a loving God embracing such limitations in order to accomplish the justification of his people is a fitting climax for the Advent season, as well as a suitable transition to the Christmas season.

Another sermonic possibility is to place the emphasis on the conclusion of the Advent season. From this perspective, the birth of Jesus can be seen as the fulfillment of the eschatological prophecies which have constituted the lessons for the last three weeks. From this perspective, the important part of the lesson is a focus on the Advent prophecies and the ways in which they are fulfilled. Of particular importance is the manner in which the prophecy about "Emmanuel" is actually fulfilled at the conclusion of this gospel.

Alternatively, it is possible to focus on Joseph as the subject of a sermon. Joseph is an interesting figure, a righteous man who can be thought of as law-abiding (the Jewish Law), or kind and compassionate, or perhaps selfish and proud, unwilling to be embarrassed by an unfaithful wife and unwilling to have an unfaithful woman as his wife (in a striking contrast to the prophet Hosea). Joseph also works quite well as a sample or prototype of most of us. We like to think of ourselves as kind and compassionate, but when we are faced with a situation that challenges us, we find it convenient to fall back to a "law-abiding" position that masks a basically selfish course of action.

Miracle Two

A Man Born Blind

The Text

As he walked along, he saw a man blind from birth. His disciples asked him, "Rabbi, who sinned, this man or his parents, that he was born blind?" Jesus answered, "Neither this man nor his parents sinned; he was born blind so that God's works might be revealed in him. We must work the works of him who sent me while it is day; night is coming when no one can work. As long as I am in the world, I am the light of the world." When he had said this, he spat on the ground and made mud with the saliva and spread the mud on the man's eyes, saying to him, "Go, wash in the pool of Siloam" (which means Sent). Then he went and washed and came back able to see.

The neighbors and those who had seen him before as a beggar began to ask, "Is this not the man who used to sit and beg?" Some were saying, "It is he." Others were saying, "No, but it is someone like him." He kept saying, "I am the man." But they kept asking him, "Then how were your eyes opened?" He answered, "The man called Jesus made mud, spread it on my eyes, and said to me, 'Go to Siloam and wash.' Then I went and washed and received my sight." They said to him, "Where is he?" He said, "I do not know."

They brought to the Pharisees the man who had formerly been blind. Now it was a sabbath day when Jesus made the mud and opened his eyes. Then the Pharisees also began to ask him how he had received his sight. He said to them, "He put mud on my eyes.

Then I washed, and now I see." Some of the Pharisees said, "This man is not from God, for he does not observe the sabbath." But others said, "How can a man who is a sinner perform such signs?" And they were divided. So they said again to the blind man, "What do you say about him? It was your eyes he opened." He said, "He is a prophet."

The Jews did not believe that he had been blind and had received his sight until they called the parents of the man who had received his sight and asked them, "Is this your son, who you say was born blind? How then does he now see?" His parents answered, "We know that this is our son, and that he was born blind; but we do not know how it is that now he sees, nor do we know who opened his eyes. Ask him; he is of age. He will speak for himself." His parents said this because they were afraid of the Jews; for the Jews had already agreed that anyone who confessed Jesus to be the Messiah would be put out of the synagogue. Therefore his parents said, "He is of age; ask him."

So for the second time they called the man who had been blind, and they said to him, "Give glory to God! We know that this man is a sinner." He answered, "I do not know whether he is a sinner. One thing I do know, that though I was blind, now I see." They said to him, "What did he do to you? How did he open your eyes?" He answered them, "I have told you already, and you would not listen. Why do you want to hear it again? Do you also want to become his disciples?" Then they reviled him, saying, "You are his disciple, but we are disciples of Moses. We know that God has spoken to Moses, but as for this man, we do not know where he comes from." The man answered, "Here is an astonishing thing! You do not know where he comes from, and yet he opened my eyes. We know that God does not listen to sinners, but he does listen to one who worships him and obeys his will. Never since the world began has it been heard that anyone opened the eyes of a person born blind. If this man were not from God, he could do nothing." They answered him, "You were born

entirely in sins, and are you trying to teach us?" And
they drove him out.

    Jesus heard that they had driven him out, and when
he found him, he said, "Do you believe in the Son of
Man?" He answered, "And who is he, sir? Tell me, so
that I may believe in him." Jesus said to him, "You
have seen him, and the one speaking with you is he."
He said, "Lord, I believe." And he worshiped him.

    Jesus said, "I came into this world for judgment
so that those who do not see may see, and those who
do see may become blind." Some of the Pharisees near
him heard this and said to him, "Surely we are not
blind, are we?" Jesus said to them, "If you were blind,
you would not have sin. But now that you say, 'We see,'
your sin remains."

This is the story of a miracle that is important mostly as the beginning of the real action of the story. Most often the miracle itself is the centerpiece of the story, but in this instance the focus is on people's reaction to the man who was healed, not the healing itself.

This can make the lesson easier as a subject for a sermon by providing an alternative to a miraculous healing which can easily be dismissed. A focus on the reactions of the audience can translate quite easily into a contemporary view of modern reactions to Jesus and the stories we hear of his actions.

Further, it is possible to consider this miracle story as John presents it as an allegory of the mission of Jesus. Many elements of the story are strikingly meaningful, leading to the idea that John presents it as holding more meaning than we expect to find in a simple story. It is quite likely that the details have been heightened to present a second, allegorical level of meaning for the readers and hearers of this text.

Finally, this lesson comes on the Fourth Sunday In Lent. As a season of great solemnity and somberness, Lent stands largely alone. Advent, in modern usage, often follows the Lenten lead, but the general tenor of the secular festivities at the time usually undermines an effort to maintain the solemnity. Lent, coming at a time of the year which is often characterized by dreary weather and a dearth of holidays, has less secular competition in establishing a mood of solemnity.

Sundays, as commemorations of Easter, are not counted as part of the forty days of Lent. In the liturgical tradition, Lenten fasts are punctuated by relief on Sundays, which results in the fact that an accurate liturgical understanding often confuses those not familiar with the traditional interpretation of the season. The Fourth Sunday In Lent is, traditionally, a day for a more celebratory worship. Often known as *Laetare* or Refreshment Sunday, the mood of this Sunday is less solemn and more joyful than the other Sundays of this season, a theme of this day which is somewhat muted in this lesson, but still present.

About The Text

This is one of the miracles of the Gospel of John, likely derived from a source commonly known as the Gospel of Signs. The liturgical calendar picks up the last three signs of this text in this year, with this being the fifth of the seven signs; the raising of Lazarus being the sixth, and the entry into Jerusalem being the concluding sign. Even though the Johannine use of the signs source is somewhat obscured by the insertion of the Marcan account of the entry into Jerusalem, the general outline is still apparent here.

Most commentators are quite clear that the text of the gospel has been modified and edited into its present form, in large part to make the story better able to serve the evangelist's purposes. Those purposes are highlighted in the sermonic possibilities listed below.

Words

who sinned — The question posed by the disciples is very much the sort of question that might be asked by students of a teacher for clarification. The question also assumes the general understanding of that time and of many people before and since, namely that blindness, and other physical deformities, illnesses, and even financial and relational problems are the direct result of sinful conduct. This attitude is based in a variety of traditions, some Jewish,

32

others from other religious traditions, which speak to the appealing nature of a cause and effect understanding of individual problems — sinful behavior leads to physical punishment. One source of the tradition is in the tractate *On the Sabbath* among the writings of the Talmud, which explains that there is no death without sin, no punishment without guilt.

This is quite a logical question to ask, therefore, about a man born blind. By virtue of his disability, the blind man is the very image of sinfulness (v. 34). The only question seems to be, "Who is the author of the sin, the man or his parents?"

The possibility of sinning before birth was likely regarded at the time as a probable cause, even if written sources discussing this possibility seem to date somewhat later than the life of Jesus. What is not being considered is the possibility of a sinful previous life or some sort of transmigration of sinful souls, which was absurd in the Judaism of the time, even if it was a part of the philosophical discussions of the time. It has been suggested that these absurdities might have been precisely what the question was meant to imply, so that the answer of Jesus could highlight the absurdity of the dogmatic understanding of the effects of sinful behavior.

spat — The Greek verb used here is also an example of onomatopoeia in the original. The root form is *ptuo*, which certainly emulates a common sound of expectoration.

Siloam (which means Sent) — With a certain level of irony, the one who was sent by God (v. 4), in turn, sends the blind man to the Pool of Siloam, the name of which is said to mean "sent." The name refers to the water in the pool, which was "sent" into the city of Jerusalem from the spring Gihon. Thus, the Pool of Siloam contained "sent" water; water which did not originate there.

The explanations, of both the reason for the man's birth defect and the name of the pool are regarded as editorial additions by the evangelist, which serve as clear indications that the story has a deeper meaning, to the point that it can be considered as an allegory for the sacrament of baptism. In this instance, the point seems to be that the washing of baptism allows Christians to see more clearly than even those who have been raised with the Word of God as disciples of Moses.

I am — In Exodus 3:15 Moses inquires of the burning bush what name he should use when the people back in Egypt ask who sent him to them. The voice from the bush responds, in the Septuagint, "*ego emi.*" This is the emphatic form in Greek, including the pronoun *ego*, which can also be assumed as part of the verb *emi*. It is stated for effect.

In the New Testament the phrase *ego emi* appears 48 times, with fully half of the appearances being found in the Gospel of John (24 of 48). About half of the remaining occurrences are found in the other gospels, with the remaining instances being found in Acts and Revelation. The phrase is usually assumed to signify, particularly in John, Jesus's claim to divinity, or, at the least, to the role of a divinely inspired messenger. Here, in verse 9, the term is used not by Jesus, however, but by the man born blind.

In verses 4 and 5, Jesus responds to the disciples' question with a phrase that sounds similar, but which is only the verb form in the Greek. The pronoun is not explicitly stated in Jesus' words, leading to the conclusion that these uses are not intended as claims of anything by Jesus, but merely as a normal verbal usage.

The use of the phrase by the man born blind is likely attributable to the dramatic nature of the argument swirling around the man, with some of his neighbors insisting he is who he says he is, and others saying he is only someone like himself. Into this argument, one which likely is escalating to ever louder voices and perhaps into the threats of violence, the man shouts the words *ego emi!* The use of that particular phrase would almost certainly silence the argument for the moment, either due to the nature of the words or due to the emphasis implied in the construction.

the Pharisees — The most progressive party in Judaism in the time of Jesus, composed largely of lawyers and legal experts who tried to live according to the Law. While some members of this group became followers of Jesus, they are regularly reported as being in opposition to his activities, as happens here. In John it is more common for the opposition to Jesus to be described as "the Jews," but the Pharisees are also used as foils for Jesus in both John and the other gospels. The Pharisees were not as strict in their legal interpretations as the residents of Qumran seem to have been, and in fact, it seems they were regularly criticized by the Qumranites for their lax interpretations of the Law.

Sabbath day — The Sabbath was, traditionally, timed from sundown Friday to sundown Saturday. According to verse 14, Jesus broke the law of Sabbath observance twice on this occasion — first by making the mud by mixing spittle and dirt, and second by curing the man's blindness. Humanitarian considerations aside, healing on the Sabbath was forbidden unless a life was in danger. Additionally, a slightly later legal opinion included the idea that anointing an individual's eyes was not permitted on the Sabbath as well. These three breaches of the Sabbath Law, while each a serious offense, might be permissible under some interpretations, but more serious charges were made in verse 16. Here the unmentioned legal point is from Deuteronomy 13:2-6, where any worker of signs, no matter how effective, who leads people away from God is to be put to death. The subtext here is the leveling of a charge which, if proved to apply, could result in Jesus' death.

sinner — A sinner is someone who does not follow the laws of the Jews, at least as they were understood and promulgated by the Pharisees. While there are differing bases for the judgment, it is clear that both sides in the Pharisee camp judged Jesus to be a sinner. The question that divided them was what sort of sin was he most guilty of.

For what it is worth, the idea that a sinner is not able to perform signs is not exactly a tenet of the Jewish tradition. The Pharonic sorcerers imitated the signs of Aaron (Exodus 7:8-12) early plagues of Moses and Aaron (Exodus 7:22 and 8:7). Further, the implication of Deuteronomy 13:2-6 clearly indicates the ability of false prophets to work wonders, an idea confirmed by Jesus' words in Matthew 24:24.

Ask him, he is of age — In some ways this statement and the reason given for it in verse 22 call the dialog here into question. There is very little evidence of legislation which excluded followers of Christ from the synagogue in the first half of the first century. Only toward the end of the first century did such legislation take effect. This leads to questions of the historicity of the account, a concern not shared by the evangelist. In his writing, John is addressing the situation of the church at the time of composition, and adjusting conflicts to reflect the situation at the time of composition seems to be a preferred way to communicate to his readers. Historicity, at least in the modern sense, is not one of the evangelist's concerns. Aside from the statement that the man born blind is of age, i.e., thirteen years old, there is no further indication of his age.

Give glory to God! — This is really a technical term which means "Tell the truth," in the spirit of Joshua 7:9.

disciples of Moses — The phrase is somewhat difficult. It is not commonly used of rabbinic scholars, although it is used on occasion for Pharisaic scholars in opposition to Sadducean scholars. The issue here, and regularly in the synoptics, is the disparity between Moses and Jesus, who is often presented as a new Moses.

In John, the miracles are meant to prove Jesus' authority, and the issue here is that the followers of Moses are unable to discern that the Son of Man is working these signs for their benefit, so that they might believe. As he heals the blind man, the eyes of the leaders of the Jewish establishment are blind to the arrival of the Messiah. In Johannine language, when the incarnate light comes to them, they remain in the darkness.

believe in — The Greek word normally translated as *believe* is somewhat odd in its use. The word requires an object be expressed with it to express the subject of the belief. Typically this is expressed, as here, with a phrase beginning with the word "in." Belief must, according to the language, always be anchored in something or someone. The more modern concept of belief, that it is possible to believe in believing, is impossible to express in Greek.

Parallels

The Gospel of John is relatively unique. Only very brief snippets have much in common with the synoptics. This is one of the portions of John which actually does have some parallels, both internally to John 5, and to the two stories in Mark of healing a blind man (as well as the parallels to the second story in Matthew and Luke).

In John 5:1-18, 19, and 30, it is possible to see a number of similarities to the lesson. Both stories are, of course, taken from the Signs Gospel, both take place in the Jerusalem area, both involve restoring the sight of a blind man who did not ask for healing, both events took place on a Sabbath, both stories result in opposition from the Jews, and both stories involve extensive editorial additions from the evangelist.

Beyond this list of similarities, there is no reason to attempt to identify any literary parallels between the two accounts. The similarities might serve to call the independence of the two events into mild question, but it is not necessary to assume that only one miracle lies behind the two stories.

Mark 8:22-26 is the story, unique to Mark, of the two-step healing of a blind man at Bethsaida. It is interesting that the name of the village is similar to the name of the pool in John 5:2, and involves the use of spittle (John 9:6, spittle and mud) as an agent in the healing. Beyond these surface similarities, there is little more that parallels the action in John 9.

Another parallel in Mark 10:46-52 (and the parallels in Matthew 20:29-34 and Luke 18:35-45) is somewhat more interesting. While it provides no more evidence of literary parallels than the other sections already examined, it places the healing of a blind man in the area of Jericho, the last stop in Mark before the triumphal entry into Jerusalem. This chronological placement parallels John's placement in the story. In John, Jesus proceeds to Bethany, where he raises Lazarus and rests before the events of the final week. The slight delay in John does not obviate the obvious similarity in timing between the synoptic and Johannine accounts.

It is likely that the recounting of a healing story of a blind man not long before the culmination of Jesus' ministry in Jerusalem

37

was a part of the tradition from a very early date. Further, it is likely that the timing of the events reflected in John and the synoptics reflects something approaching the actual historical sequence of events.

The People

As Individuals

The man born blind is an interesting character. His age is, beyond the mere fact that he is at least thirteen, indeterminate. On the other hand, once his sight has been restored, he sees quite clearly. Without introductions, he is able to identify Jesus as the one who opened his eyes, and in verse 35 he recognizes Jesus in the flesh without, apparently, ever having seen him. The question of how he would know what Jesus looked like, considering the long-distance nature of the miracle, is a question the text does not answer, or even address.

It is reasonable to suspect that others in the crowd would supply the information to the man. In fact, it is not beyond the realm of possibility that a contingent of the crowd accompanied the man to the Pool of Siloam to observe the results of the miracle. When the man was able to see, the crowd could easily have supplied the gaps in his knowledge.

More interesting is the man's refusal to get into a theological discussion with the Pharisees until provoked. Rather than theologizing, the man sticks to the bare facts in his first interview (John 9:13-17). Even the assertion in verse 17, "He is a prophet," is somewhat ambiguous. The prophets were not noted for healing miracles, with the exception of Elijah and Elisha (and possibly Isaiah, see 38:21). What seems to be indicated here is an affirmation by the man born blind that Jesus has the divine power of a prophet.

In his second interview (John 9:24-34) the man begins in the same way, sticking entirely to the facts of the case without editorial comment. Then, in verse 27, the man is obviously tired of being the subject of a Pharisaic investigation and he flares into irony — "Do you also want to become his disciples?" The implication is

38

that the man is already a disciple of Jesus, apparently and simply by virtue of being the recipient of a healing.

The Pharisees react predictably to the jibe from the man, and he then confronts them with the central truth of the incident. The theological comments make the point of the evangelist quite clearly, and lead to yet another disparaging comment from the Pharisees before they expel him from their presence (and perhaps from the synagogue, or traditional Jewish circles as well).

After this stirring defense of the actions of Jesus and the implications of them, there is a final confrontation between Jesus and the man, in which the man is once again less than completely clear about what has happened, or at least about the identity of Jesus. Once the situation is explained to him, he quickly professes belief in Christ.

The parents of the man are actually worried about a situation that wasn't present in the time of Jesus, namely being expelled from the synagogue. It is possible that they were also somewhat concerned about another problem. At the time, the commandment to honor parents was understood to mean making provisions for a person's parents in their old age. A person was adjudged to have fulfilled the commandment when provisions were made for this support.

It is possible to hear a touch of bitterness in the parents' comment — "Ask him, he is of age" (John 9:21). If the man born blind is of age, he should be providing some support for his parents, but as someone with a disability, it is more likely that his parents were still providing some portion of support for their adult son. In this case, the problem sounds quite modern, when many grandparents suddenly find their "golden years" devoted to caring for their adult children and younger grandchildren as a matter of necessity which is imposed on them.

The Pharisees are the epitome of obstinate antagonists for Jesus. They find themselves unable to understand the basic mechanism by which a person they judge to be a sinner can perform such actions. At the conclusion of this lesson, the Pharisees are confounded and are obviously the blind ones. More than simply another disparagement of the Pharisees, this use also provides a prelude to the plot hatched in John 11:45-53, as well as an inherent explanation for the inability of Caiaphas to understand the true implications of his prophetic statement in the meeting that developed the plot (John 11:49-50). Placing the Pharisees in the larger context of this gospel provides another view of the skilled editorship and literary ability of the evangelist.

As Images And Signs
Since John 1:4, the image of light has been associated with the Word of God and Jesus. In John 1:5, a theme of this gospel is enunciated — The light shines in the darkness, and the darkness did not overcome it. And the ninth chapter of the gospel expands on that single sentence, providing a fully detailed story about the struggle between the light and darkness, complete with details of the struggle and applications to the lives of the readers (and hearers) of the lesson.

When we understand this story as an allegory, which is one way (not the only way) to understand what the evangelist is doing here, it becomes clear that Jesus, the light of the world, gives light to the man who has been living in darkness for his entire life. This miraculous event causes problems for the custodians of the Mosaic tradition (the Pharisees) because the healing takes place on the Sabbath, an obvious breach of the law. As a lawbreaker, also known as a sinner, it seems obvious to the Pharisees that the sinful man Jesus couldn't possibly have accomplished a miracle with God's blessing.

This inability to grasp the miracle as proof of Jesus' authority is a sign of the blindness of the Pharisees, a problem which is, in reality, much more serious than the physical blindness of the man who was healed. As is a common theme in Luke, and other gospels, this is a reversal of what people might expect to hear from Jesus. The "common-sense" understandings of the Pharisees are stood on end by the successful healing on the Sabbath. They, and in fact the man born blind as well, had always understood that no sinner could possibly perform such mighty acts as healing.

Starting from the fact that Jesus was clearly a sinner who had obviously broken the Sabbath Law, the Pharisees were unable to understand what was happening in the ministry of Jesus. The man born blind, on the other hand, began with his newly restored eyesight, and reasoned that because he could see, the man who had accomplished this miraculous feat had to be someone who worshiped God and obeyed his will (John 9:31). Thus, two participants, the Pharisees and the subject of the miracle, both examine the same facts and use the same assumption to arrive at totally different conclusions.

In their efforts to resolve the conflict, the Pharisees accuse the man of lying to them. They go so far as to summon the man's parents to verify his story that he was, in fact, born blind. When it checks out, all they can do is to eject the man from their fellowship. They are unable to resolve the basic problem they are facing. Their problems simply multiply as they insist on beginning with the nature of the worker of the miracle.

The man has a much simpler resolution. He can see suddenly, and he is absolutely convinced of the character of the person who caused this miracle in his life. Newly able to even see light, he is now a devoted follower of that light. All problems have been resolved when he begins with the results of the miracle.

The evaluation of Jesus as a sinner by the Pharisees might be a troublesome picture for some people. The religious authorities of his day had little or no difficulty in so labeling him, and the charges are presented here with no particularly obvious effort to refute the charges. It certainly seems possible that the need to present a perfectly sinless Jesus was not as strongly felt by the evangelist as it has been felt by some apologists after the gospel was completed.

There are two ways to understand the technical breach of the Sabbath recounted in this account, two defenses which might be offered for such behavior. The first is that offered by Mark when the disciples plucked some grain and ate it on the Sabbath. This act of harvesting was the basis for accusations by the Pharisees and the cause of a defense by Jesus based on David's actions in 1 Samuel 21:1-7. Jesus summarizes by stating that the Sabbath was made for humanity, not humanity for the Sabbath (Mark 2:27). This is a rather more relaxed attitude than that of even the Pharisees, in which the strict rules of the Sabbath observance are made secondary to the needs of people, particularly the need for healing by the man born blind in this instance.

In Matthew's version of the incident recounted by Mark, Jesus' comment on the Sabbath is omitted, but a more legalistic justification is offered. The priests in the temple are required to make a Sabbath offering (Numbers 28:9-10), which is a form of work. However, as this is the work of God, the priests are held guiltless of breaking the Sabbath (Matthew12:5). In order to do the work of God, it is, therefore, considered acceptable, or at least guiltless to break the Sabbath.

Either of these justifications might be understood in the lesson here, but neither is stated explicitly.

The Action

In The Story

The lesson begins with some interesting points. First, there is little visible connection between what comes before in John 8 and this incident. Events simply begin, with little indication of setting or effort to connect with what has gone before. This has led some to suggest the story should be found in some other location within the gospel. The story simply begins with Jesus and the disciples walking along when they happen to see a man who was blind from birth.

Another interesting point involves the initial confrontation with the man. From the miracle stories of the synoptics, most people are very used to hearing a request for healing as a prelude to the actual healing. In fact, we are so used to hearing the request that when it is not present, it is easy to assume it was really there. But, in fact, the man born blind does not ask for a miracle. In fact, whether he might have asked for one or not, from the rest of the story it is clear he has heard very little, perhaps nothing about Jesus prior to the events recounted here. And even if he had heard of him, he has no idea of which individual might be the person he has heard about.

There is no request here. Rather, the picture presented is a rather impersonal one. Jesus finds a blind man begging at the side of the road, the disciples ask a question, and Jesus heals the man's blindness. This simple act, and the day of the week on which it took place, cause two separate sets of difficulties.

First, the Pharisees, the religious authorities of the day, had substantial problems with the fact that a healing (work) took place on the Sabbath. Work is forbidden on the Sabbath, and even if humanitarian considerations make this seem a rather harsh restriction, it should be noted that acts which resulted in healing, but were required to save a life, were not forbidden. It was acts such as the one Jesus performed with the unfortunate man born blind which should, to conform to the requirements of the law, be postponed until the next day.

Much of the problem the Pharisees had has been examined previously, including the issue of a healing, by definition a manifestation of God's power, accomplished as the result of a sinful act. Further, the action took place outside the religious establishment. As the plot in John 11:45-57 is hatched and unfolds, it is the religious establishment that provides the leadership which opposes Jesus and plots and finally clamors for his death. The present incident is certainly one that encourages the Pharisaic leaders to desire the end of Jesus' ministry.

In this incident, we can profitably note that the Pharisees spend most of their time trying to shake the story of the man born blind, to prove him a liar and charlatan by interviewing his parents, and finally by having a loud argument with the man. The problem here can be seen as an effort by the Pharisees to avoid facing the real problem, the true source of their discomfort — Jesus.

In The Hearers

The second difficulty in this story is one which is basic to all the stories of miracles in the New Testament. Why are miracle stories included? In the Gospel of John, the purpose is quite clearly stated — "Jesus did this, in Cana of Galilee, and revealed his glory; and his disciples believed in him" (John 2:11). Miracles in this gospel are meant to create belief (see, for example, John 4:53b; 6:2, 14, and 30). The difficulty here is encapsulated in Jesus' answer to the disciples' question — "He was born blind so that God's

43

works might be revealed in him" (John 9:3). This answer brings to mind a rather unflattering picture of God, who creates people with severe deformities and disabilities so they will be available later as subjects for demonstrations of God's power. This is a rather dismal view of God, and not a very comforting one. Suffering and personal anguish are not taken into account. People are discounted and diminished to the point of being mere props to be used to make a point.

The theological point here is strictly limited to miracles as a cause for belief. In the context of this lesson, the miracle and the reactions of the characters in the story emphasize the various ways in which belief can be brought forth. Not all the reactions are a growing belief in Jesus. Not that this disparity of reactions is unexpected in John (see John 6:60-71 for another example of this tendency). In many ways, this story is not meant to be an historical account of individual people, but a story which illustrates the way belief works itself out in life. As such, it is not appropriate to the push the story too far and demand a humanitarian understanding of all the characters in the story.

The Sermon

Illustrations

Many stories and sayings remind us of some of the worst aspects of controversy. Here are two with a country accent:

A country philosopher once pointed out that people are willing to meet each other half way; the trouble is most people are pretty poor judges of distance.

And then there was the small, rural church that faced a motion in the annual meeting to buy a new chandelier. Only one man protested. He complained, "First, not a one of us can even spell that word. Second, nobody here can play it, even if we did get it. And third, what we really need in this church is more light."

Speaking of light, a theme of this lesson:

A pilot was flying his small, single-engine plane in the late afternoon. Before he could line up his approach to the small, unattended field where he planned to land, darkness had settled in and he was unable to see the field. For a time the pilot circled the field, trying to think of some way to land the plane before he ran out of gas.

Finally, as the gas gauge settled toward the E, a man on the ground heard the plane and realized the problem. He drove his car to the field, drove up and down the runway, and then parked at the far end, with his headlights illuminating the airstrip to guide the pilot to a safe landing.

Perhaps the issue of this lesson might be understood as the difficulty of the Pharisees with the challenge of Jesus to their world:

Consider a child who was riding his bicycle and was hit by a car. When people hear of the accident, they don't ask what happened to the bicycle, they ask about the child. At the best, the current world situation is our bicycle, and we have been in an accident. The issue isn't the condition of the bicycle, or the condition of the world; the issue is our spiritual health, our spiritual well being after we have been over run by sin.

Then there is also the comment from the late philosopher Eric Hoffer, "Taking a new step, uttering a new word is what people fear most."

Approaches To Preaching

As unusual an approach as it might be, the fact that the miracle precedes belief in this case is worth consideration. Belief is not a prerequisite for salvation in this case. And, as much as we might try to establish a variety of requirements for membership in the church, and membership as a requirement for salvation, one aspect of this lesson is clearly contrary to institutional desires to make some sort of commitment a prerequisite that can only be accomplished in or by the church.

On Laetare Sunday the reaction of the man born blind is also worth consideration. Not only his faith, but also his natural reaction of joy and excitement at suddenly being able to see for the first time in his life (even if underplayed in the text) fit the traditional mood of the Sunday quite well.

Related to the issue of requirements, there is the matter of baptism. The lesson does have at least a thread of sacramental recognition in the requirement to wash in the Pool of Siloam. This has been recognized as a possible reference to the sacrament of baptism for many centuries. And the general requirement of membership in the church of having been baptized is certainly minimal at best.

Further, the evangelist's purpose in this lesson certainly includes the exposition of the ways the light triumphs over darkness. There are many ways this occurs, and not all of them are ways that the religious establishment finds appropriate, as the Pharisees demonstrate in this lesson. Baptism as the act that opens our eyes to see the light of Christ, and to see our salvation is another way to proclaim the Word from this lesson.

The miracle in this lesson is an excuse for the discussion of the reactions of the various witnesses to the events. The man born blind responds with, understandably, joy and faith in Jesus. The Pharisees respond with disbelief and a desire to disprove the events. The man's parents respond with a desire not to be involved, a sort of apathy. The other characters, who are largely off the stage in the story, can be thought of in a variety of ways. Likely gossipy as they follow and observe the main characters, perhaps disbelieving as they follow the man to the Pool of Siloam to see if he is really cured, maybe even a little bloodthirsty like the spectators at a bullfight or car race who are waiting for the accident they hope will come.

Finally, Jesus describes his coming as "judgment" (John 9:39), a reversal of the current order of things. As the events have worked out, the man born blind sees, and the Pharisees have demonstrated their spiritual blindness. The judgment continues to this day, and confronts people all the time. When those who do not see are enabled to see, and those who see become blind, the issue is one which resonates in much of the biblical tradition, a topsy-turvy reordering of the order of things that seem so commonsensical. Instead, the blind see, and the sighted are blind. And that question confronts us all — do we see or are we blind?

Miracle Three

Raising Lazarus

The Text

*Now a certain man was ill, Lazarus of Bethany, the vil-
lage of Mary and her sister Martha. Mary was the one
who anointed the Lord with perfume and wiped his feet
with her hair; her brother Lazarus was ill. So the sisters sent a message to Jesus, "Lord, he whom you love
is ill." But when Jesus heard it, he said, "This illness
does not lead to death; rather it is for God's glory, so
that the Son of God may be glorified through it." Accordingly, though Jesus loved Martha and her sister and
Lazarus, after having heard that Lazarus was ill, he
stayed two days longer in the place where he was.*

*Then after this he said to the disciples, "Let us go to
Judea again." The disciples said to him, "Rabbi, the
Jews were just now trying to stone you, and are you going there again?" Jesus answered, "Are there not twelve
hours of daylight? Those who walk during the day do
not stumble, because they see the light of this world. But
those who walk at night stumble, because the light is not
in them." After saying this, he told them, "Our friend
Lazarus has fallen asleep, but I am going there to awaken
him." The disciples said to him, "Lord, if he has fallen
asleep, he will be all right." Jesus, however, had been
speaking about his death, but they thought that he was
referring merely to sleep. Then Jesus told them plainly,
"Lazarus is dead. For your sake I am glad I was not
there, so that you may believe. But let us go to him."
Thomas, who was called the Twin, said to his fellow disciples, "Let us also go, that we may die with him."*

When Jesus arrived, he found that Lazarus had already been in the tomb four days. Now Bethany was near Jerusalem, some two miles away, and many of the Jews had come to Martha and Mary to console them about their brother. When Martha heard that Jesus was coming, she went and met him, while Mary stayed at home. Martha said to Jesus, "Lord, if you had been here, my brother would not have died. But even now I know that God will give you whatever you ask of him." Jesus said to her, "Your brother will rise again." Martha said to him, "I know that he will rise again in the resurrection on the last day." Jesus said to her, "I am the resurrection and the life. Those who believe in me, even though they die, will live, and everyone who lives and believes in me will never die. Do you believe this?" She said to him, "Yes, Lord, I believe that you are the Messiah, the Son of God, the one coming into the world."

When she had said this, she went back and called her sister Mary, and told her privately, "The Teacher is here and is calling for you." And when she heard it, she got up quickly and went to him. Now Jesus had not yet come to the village, but was still at the place where Martha had met him. The Jews who were with her in the house, consoling her, saw Mary get up quickly and go out. They followed her because they thought that she was going to the tomb to weep there. When Mary came where Jesus was and saw him, she knelt at his feet and said to him, "Lord, if you had been here, my brother would not have died."

When Jesus saw her weeping, and the Jews who came with her also weeping, he was greatly disturbed in spirit and deeply moved. He said, "Where have you laid him?" They said to him, "Lord, come and see." Jesus began to weep. So the Jews said, "See how he loved him!" But some of them said, "Could not he who opened the eyes of the blind man have kept this man from dying?"

Then Jesus, again greatly disturbed, came to the tomb. It was a cave, and a stone was lying against it.

Jesus said, "Take away the stone." Martha, the sister
of the dead man, said to him, "Lord, already there is a
stench because he has been dead four days." Jesus said
to her, "Did I not tell you that if you believed, you would
see the glory of God?" So they took away the stone.
And Jesus looked upward and said, "Father, I thank
you for having heard me. I knew that you always hear
me, but I have said this for the sake of the crowd stand-
ing here, so that they may believe that you sent me."
When he had said this, he cried with a loud voice,
"Lazarus, come out!" The dead man came out, his
hands and feet bound with strips of cloth, and his face
wrapped in a cloth. Jesus said to them, "Unbind him,
and let him go."
Many of the Jews therefore, who had come with
Mary and had seen what Jesus did, believed in him.

It is, perhaps, ironic that a lesson which has been the subject of
as much critical discussion as this one has should be found here,
on the eve of two of the busiest weeks of the year in the average
parish. Even the week of Christmas is usually not as packed with
extra worship services, additional sermons to prepare, and other
activities as are the two weeks immediately preceding the celebration of Easter.

And yet, here is a lesson which has been the subject of substantial discussion, much of it centering on the very basic question
of whether the story is a dramatic construction of the evangelist or
if it has a basis in the events of the life of Jesus. The scholars seem
to be quite divided in their assessment, which can add yet another
burden to the harried preacher when it is time to prepare the sermon for this Sunday. When so much else requires attention, it is
necessary to face the intellectual rigors of sorting out divergent
scholarly opinions in order to prepare the weekly sermon.

The main difficulty seems to be that the story of such a spec-
tacular miracle would, logically, be certain of inclusion in the synoptic gospels, if it were known to those evangelists. And, as important as the family of Lazarus, Mary, and Martha appear to be (both
in John and Luke), there is little reason why it would not be known

at least to Luke if the story actually happened. The argument is, of course, not as strong as it sounds as it rests on the silence of the synoptics, not on any demonstrable comments.

The story certainly does fill an important place in the fourth gospel as well as in the Lenten season in this year (John 11:32-44 is also appointed for All Saints' Day in Cycle B). The raising of Lazarus is the event which is the climax and conclusion of Jesus' public ministry. After this Jesus retreats to wait for the coming of the Passover, his hour, and the climax of his life (John 11:54).

This purpose is retained in the sequence of lessons in this year, in the lessons appointed for Lent 4, this Sunday, Passion Sunday, Maundy Thursday, Good Friday, and the Resurrection Of The Lord. Even though the third Gospel Lesson of the sequence is taken from Mark, the events are parallel to those of John, thus retaining the dramatic Johannine building to the absolute climax of the Good News with the readings of Easter, which is the true basis for the other lessons in the cycle.

The lesson today, for all the controversy which has swirled around it, serves as the perfect transition from the public ministry to the Passion, and as a dramatic foreshadowing of the events of the coming Holy Week.

About The Text

In fact, the arguments over the factuality of this lesson are generally not something which needs to be mentioned from the pulpit. Perhaps in a study group such questions might be explored, but they have little place in a sermon.

This lengthy lesson might be an excuse for a shortening of the proclamation on this day, which is understandable, if lamentable. The various strands of the gospel to this point are brought together by a master and the stage is expertly set for what is to come. The preacher, to do justice to this lesson, should make the effort to do the same. At the least, we are approaching the end of the journey of Lent, and as we travel up to Jerusalem for the concluding events, this lesson affords a chance to prepare for the hectic events to come.

Words

ill — The word used here is, literally, weak, and it is used in the New Testament both in a literal sense, as here where *weak* is taken physically, and read as *ill*, and more figuratively (in some translations) in places like Acts 20:35, where the sense is *economically weak*, or *poor*.

Mary was — The word is actually *is* (an example of an historical present usage), but has been changed to simplify the tenses after the centuries have made the past more appropriate. It would seem that the evangelist is identifying a person known to his readers, or at least a family whose ancestors (of a generation or two ago) were known by reputation to those who heard his gospel.

who anointed the Lord — This identification is out of place here, as the anointing doesn't actually occur in this gospel until John 12:3. Further, the title *Lord* is an uncommon one in John. It may be that this identification has been taken from a source, or perhaps John is influenced at this point by Luke, with whom he seems to have been somewhat familiar.

glorified — This word, which incorporates an important concept in this gospel, has at least a double meaning in this saying of Jesus. It certainly has the usual meaning of the rationale for an unusual circumstance which will be utilized to show the working of God in this world ("so the Son of God may be glorified") and to bring people to believe in Jesus (which occurs in 11:45).

In addition, the events that unfold in these verses also serve to point to the cross and the glorification of Jesus on the cross. Further, the crucifixion is presented by the evangelist as the direct result of Jesus' public ministry in general, and the miracle recounted here specifically.

light of this world — This term brings back the themes of this gospel and connects them directly to this incident. Further, in the sequence of the church year, this also harks back to last week's lesson. The concept here is also double-edged. First, Jesus points out that the light is still present, which is taken to mean that the time for Jesus' public ministry still has some period to run. While there is time, Jesus continues to minister where he finds a need. In addition to this obvious interpretation, the application of the phrase here also points to the cross, where Jesus illuminates the world through his death.

fallen asleep — Most people understand this term as a euphemism for death. In the New Testament the Greek word translated here is used both as a euphemism and in the literal sense of sleep. The term is also used in Sirach 46:19 as a euphemism. Here the disciples misunderstand euphemism and assume the literal use of the term is meant. This leads Jesus to state quite clearly that Lazarus has died. Even today, the use of euphemism is quite common, particularly when referring to death. The list can be quite long, and includes terms such as "passed on," "gone," and "departed."

Thomas — *Didymus* in Greek, Thomas is the Greek form of the Hebrew name which means twin. In Matthew (10:3), Mark (3:18), Luke (6:15), and Acts (1:13), the name appears only in lists of the disciples. It is only in the Gospel of John that Thomas merits more than a passing mention.

In John's Gospel, Thomas is, perhaps most notably, the disciple who doubts the first appearance of the resurrected Christ. Previously he is mentioned in this lesson and in John 14:5, where he responds to Jesus' long comments with a statement of his ignorance. From all three of these incidents, it seems almost as if Thomas has taken over some of the actions we expect, based on the generally more familiar accounts of the synoptics, to be credited to Peter.

Thomas' identity is not completely clear. One suggestion is that his name comes from the fact that he was the twin of Jesus. This suggestion is found most clearly in the gnostic writings (see *The Acts of Thomas, Gospel of Thomas,* and *The Book of Thomas the Contender*). The last named source includes sayings from Jesus directed to "Brother Thomas," which might be understood as an acknowledgment of the familial relationship. All three gnostic writings also refer to Thomas as *Judas Thomas*. This has led some to suggest, based further on some of the details in the gnostic sources, that Judas' betrayal might have roots in a sort of sibling rivalry.

Thomas is the traditional founder of the Indian church, but only after trying mightily to beg off of the assignment. Eventually he goes to India and gives his life in the founding of the Indian Christian church (known traditionally as the Thomist Church). All these details are, of course, traditional and legendary at best.

Thomas' comment in this lesson is both a misunderstanding and a prophecy. As it stands, Thomas' suggestion that the disciples should join Jesus in his imminent death in Jerusalem clearly indicates his misunderstanding of the events Jesus is talking about. In this instance Caiaphas is the better prophet (John 11:50). However, after Jesus' death and resurrection the words of Thomas describe the life of Christians quite accurately, particularly for those Christians who are preparing for baptism during the Lenten season.

fellow disciples — This term is a *hapax legomenon*, and perhaps embodies a flash of jealousy in response to Jesus' description in verse 11 of Lazarus as "our friend." In Greek the word used of Lazarus is *philos*, which is better translated as "beloved," which might be the source of jealous feelings.

to console them — The Jews, according to verse 8, have been seeking to stone Jesus. Here, however, the Jews are merely the people who have come from Jerusalem to comfort the family on the death of Lazarus. There is no evidence that there is any sinister reason for the presence of the mourners, and nothing sinister about their actions until after the miracle actually takes place. Clearly, these are not necessarily the Jews who are trying to stone Jesus.

The mourning for a death at this time usually took place after the burial. In large part this was dictated by both the laws of the Jewish tradition and practical considerations. Embalming was not commonly practiced among the Jews of this time and place, and it did not take long for a body to begin to smell. Thus, a rapid burial was the norm, and the mourning took place after the body had been placed in the tomb.

55

There are those who point at these mourners and suggest that in the original version of the story, as taken from the Signs Gospel, Jesus met the mourners immediately after the burying of Lazarus. The account here has been edited by the evangelist, apparently to add to the dramatic nature of the story.

I am — In the lesson of last week, the man born blind used this phrase, and it's significance was examined. Here the phrase is also used, this time by Jesus, and here it is an *ego emi* phrase, and provides a self-revelation of Jesus' divinity and nature. At the conclusion of his statement, Jesus questions Martha's acceptance of his revelation.

I believe — Martha's response to Jesus' question begins with the same formulation normally used to introduce a creedal statement. Martha's answer is composed of three statements which, taken together can be regarded as a creedal form.

Privately — It isn't clear why Martha approached Mary privately, except to direct the reader's attention to Mary, and to separate her from the Jews around her. Even this statement is not evidence that the Jews are enemies of Jesus in this context. The statement also implies that Jesus asked for Mary's presence at the tomb, but that is not explicitly stated.

The Teacher — This seems to be the term used by the followers of Jesus to refer to him when he was not physically present. The term is largely another way of speaking of Jesus as a Rabbi (a Hebrew word usually taken to mean *teacher*), as is established in John 1:38 and 3:2. The use of "Teacher" as a title of respect is found in other areas of the Jewish tradition at the time of Jesus, perhaps most notably in the use of the title "Teacher of Righteousness" by the residents of Qumran to refer to their most important leader and interpreter of scripture.

greatly disturbed in spirit — The word translated as *greatly disturbed* appears only five times in the New Testament. The root

56

meaning seems to include some element of anger, which is not readily apparent in the translation. In verse 33, the word is modified by *in spirit*, while in verse 38 it is modified by *in himself.* In both cases, there is an element of anger mingled with other disturbances in Jesus' emotional state.

The exact cause, or target of Jesus' anger here is not clear. The Jews have been suggested as targets because of their obstinate refusal to show faith in Jesus, but this is not clearly stated in the text. It is important to note that in the Gospel of John, the theme of Jewish hypocrisy, which is employed in the synoptics, is absent. Thus, to remain true to the spirit of the gospel, it is important not to label Jewish hypocrisy as the target of Jesus' anger.

Another possible source of Jesus' anger might be the simple human response to a death that puts people Jesus was close to through an emotional ringer. While this suggestion likely involves a modern reading of the recounted events, it does provide an potentially interesting tension as a key to understanding Jesus' reaction.

a stench — Martha's comment about the potential stench brings up a variety of issues. The first is the question of funerary practices at that time among the Jews. If Lazarus had been embalmed, then not only would the stench be lessened, but the miraculous nature of these events would be greatly enhanced. While there is not a complete consensus on the details of burial customs at the time, embalming does not seem to have been the common practice at this time.

The bandages that hindered Lazarus' appearance from the tomb are sometimes suggested as an evidence of the use of embalming, but they are more likely to be the typical wrappings applied to a body at the time.

Another important aspect of this comment is the rather blunt intrusion of reality it represents. Suddenly, in the midst of the highlight of the sequence of signs, we find this expression of unsavory reality. It is a reminder that these events happen in the midst of a real tragedy for the family, with a Jesus who shares many of the feelings of grief and rage at the events themselves.

I thank you — The Greek word translated here is often used, at least in Christian writings, as the technical term for the community meal — the eucharist. The Greek term, *eucharisto soy*, is used only with reference to the feeding of the 5,000 in John, where it has a clear reference to the eucharist. Here there is no such reference, which points out the tendency in Christian usage to maintain both the simple use ("thank you") and the technical sense ("eucharist") of the word.

bound with strips of cloth — The use of strips of cloth, while not an indication of embalming, has caused some questions. One image that is brought up is that of a binding which wraps the arms with the body and the feet together, almost as if the binding was that of a classic Egyptian mummy. Another possibility is of a looser binding, with the legs and arms being bound independently.

While clearly the second sort of binding would make the physical details easier to fit together, the idea of binding the legs together should not be dismissed entirely. Consider the fashion, which resurfaces on occasion, of a dress that ends below the knees, with a small diameter of hem. This often causes the person wearing such a garment to shuffle along rather than walking with a more natural stride.

Parallels

Once again, the Gospel of John does not provide an exact parallel to incidents recounted in the synoptics, but it does present echoes of familiar stories from that source. More than simply similarities which lead to academic questions, in this case the similarities lead to rather serious questions.

In Mark 14:3-9 (and in the parallel accounts in Matthew 26:6-13 and Luke 7:37-50), an unnamed woman anoints Jesus. Luke places this event in an unnamed town quite early in his account, Mark and Matthew set the story in Bethany just before the final Passover begins. Many commentators point to this event, at least in the chronology provided by Mark, as the anointing of Jesus which was required prior to burial. Tradition has suggested that Mary was the person who anointed Jesus' feet in this story, but there is no basis in the texts to back up the traditional version. Other traditions identify Mary with Mary Magdalene, but, again, there is no corroboration of this supposition beyond the identity of names.

In Luke 10:38-42 we are introduced to Mary and Martha, two sisters from Bethany. In this story, Martha is the more active sister. Mary chooses to sit at the feet of Jesus, but Martha is bustling around, preparing food and serving her guests. A complaint brings forth the observation that Mary has chosen the better part. While her activities are not as prominent, Mary is given credit for having a better understanding of Jesus' presence and significance.

In John's account, Mary's understanding is more rudimentary than Martha's. In John 11:27 Martha makes a confession that echoes that of Peter at Caesarea Philippi. In John 11:32, Mary is only able to see that Jesus could have prevented Lazarus' death, not reversed it. Thus, compared to the account in Luke, Martha's understanding has deepened, while Mary's understanding has receded.

This identification of a parallel between Luke and John assumes that John knew at least portions of Luke's Gospel, and used those portions which he found to be most pertinent. An extension of this Johannine awareness is the possibility that this story is an example of a parable becoming an event. In Luke 16:19-31 is the story of a poor man named Lazarus who died and the developments after his death (and the death of a local rich man). The story ends with a rejection of a plea for Lazarus to return from the dead and confront the surviving brothers of the rich man. Luke 16:31 states, "If they do not listen to Moses and the prophets, neither will they be convinced even if someone rises from the dead."

Some commentators, particularly those who seek to eliminate the miraculous elements from the gospels, suggest that this idea has been made into the story as John presents it. As the name Lazarus appears only in the Lucan story and chapter 11 of John, the supposition has been given some credence.

An alternative suggestion involves the possibility that the synopticists had some knowledge of John, or at least of his sources, in this case the Gospel of Signs. Or, assuming the story reflects an actual incident, the situation gives rise to questions about why the raising of Lazarus is conspicuously absent from the synoptic accounts.

It has been suggested that the story was not mentioned in an effort to protect the family of Mary, Martha, and Lazarus from retribution by the local authorities. Unfortunately this suggestion includes a number of further implausibilities, including the basic idea that such a notable event and the local participants in the action would, within a generation, fade completely from local memory. This is not particularly likely, especially in a village where descendants of the participants (if not the elderly participants themselves) were still residing.

Another possible explanation for the synoptic omission of this story is that the source was a story with anonymous characters. In this case, John would have made the identification of the characters as Mary, Martha, and Lazarus. Clearly, from John 11:1, the evangelist expected that the hearers of the story would know (or at least know of) the family. There is often a tendency to identify known people with anonymous characters in stories which could certainly have taken place here.

All of this leads to some significant questions, perhaps the most important of which is the essential historicity of the miracle. In the synoptics the stories of the raising of the dead (Mark 5:21-43 and parallels in Matthew 9:18-26 and Luke 8:40-56, also Luke 7:11-16) come earlier and are not highlighted as the culmination of the public ministry of Christ as is the raising of Lazarus in John. Further, in the fourth gospel the elements of the story have been arranged to emphasize the dramatic nature of the story. Jesus' delay in arriving, Martha's comments, and the fact of the completed burial all add to the dramatic intensity of the story. With this clear tendency to heighten the elements of the story, the entire story is sometimes questioned. While there is no corroboration for this miracle from the synoptics, there is little reason to doubt the basic narrative comes from an historical incident.

Finally, Jesus' question about the location of Lazarus' burial site is precisely the information that will be sought about the body of Jesus later in this gospel. John 20:2, 13, and 15 all involve questions about where the body might be found, particularly when it is not where it is expected to be.

The People

As Individuals

Mary and Martha are already known from the Gospel of Luke, and expected to be known to those who hear this story in John. Luke 10:38-42 presents the episode of Jesus visiting the home of Martha and Mary, and Martha is very busy with the typical labors of a woman in those days (and also, quite frequently, in present time), while Mary sits at Jesus' feet and listens to his teaching. In response to Martha's complaints about Mary shirking her duties, Jesus rebukes her and defends Mary's choice as the better one.

Here Martha is once again bustling around, and the more forward of the sisters, but the relative understanding of the faith on the part of the sisters has changed. When Martha is pressed by Jesus to go beyond the understandings current in the Judaism of the day (expressed in 11:24), she makes a confession of Jesus as the Christ, the Son of God (a messianic term), and as the one coming into the world (which harkens back to the description of John the Baptizer in John 1:15, 27, and 30). This confession is at least as appropriate as that of Peter (earlier) at Caesarea Philippi, and seems to be made publicly, as opposed to Peter's, which was made only before Jesus and the disciples.

Mary, on the other hand, is only able to echo Martha's opening statement (11:21), and she never grows past that statement (11:32). In this story it is Martha whose faith has deepened and matured, while Mary remains with the faith both Martha and she began with.

Lazarus is, at most, a rather shadowy figure in this story. The name comes from Eleazer (God helps), which might have been a consideration in selecting a name for this story, but likely had nothing to do with selecting the name. There is no indication of his position in the family (younger or older brother), but he is most likely the guardian of his sisters at the time of his death. His death would seem, thus, to bring with it the specter of economic difficulties for the women.

Clearly he was the object of much affection from both his sisters and Jesus, and his sudden death was an emotionally wrenching time for all of them. This makes the actions of Jesus in delaying his

61

departure appear somewhat callous, even knowing that the final result would be the restoration of Lazarus to life. It is usually thought that Lazarus was merely restored to life, not resurrected. Hence, he could look forward to another death eventually.

Jesus' actions in this story are somewhat questionable, particularly the delay in heading for Bethany. Even though the delay does heighten the impact of the eventual miracle, it also subjects at least the sisters and the mourners with them to the emotional turmoil of experiencing a loved one's death. Jesus also has an emotional reaction to the death of Lazarus (11:35), even though the event was not only completely expected but also soon to be reversed.

The mention of the four days Lazarus has been in the tomb (11:39) has led to efforts to determine Jesus' location prior to miracle, but such attempts are generally futile. The comment does serve to remind readers that preparing the body for burial was the task of women, so both sisters were quite sure Lazarus was dead, as they had, almost certainly, prepared the body. This is a subtle reminder of the absolute verification of this miracle. Those who had prepared the body, and thus were absolutely certain the man was dead, were witnesses to the raising of Lazarus.

As Images And Signs

This is the climactic miracle of the Gospel of Signs. And, as are all the miracles in that source, it is meant to bring people to faith. John 11:45 points out the success of the miracle in that regard. This miracle is followed by the entry into Jerusalem and the Passion account. If these were originally part of the Gospel of Signs, then this climactic miracle was also a transition in the original text from the public ministry that brought people to faith, and the passion that brought Jesus to glorification.

Lazarus can be seen as a symbol of baptism. He submitted to the death and the days in the tomb, and then was raised to a new life by Jesus. Baptism is a symbolic death to our old life and a rebirth into a new life in Christ, which is precisely what happens with Lazarus. Inclusion of a lesson that refers to the Sacrament of Baptism is highly appropriate in the waning days of Lent. The season derived from the period during which catechumens of the early

62

church prepared for reception into the church through the sacrament.

Further, many assume that Lazarus was still dead when he came out of the tomb. This is sometimes known as the "miracle within a miracle," based on the understanding possible in the text that Lazarus was only restored to life with Jesus' final words, "Unbind him, and let him go" (John 11:44). In saying these words, according to this conception of events, Jesus is commanding death itself to let Lazarus go so he may return to life.

A very important theme in this gospel surfaces in this lesson. This is the idea of Jesus' glorification, which is first mentioned here in 11:4. The reference here is to a future event, which we are well aware is the event of the crucifixion. The theme is reintroduced in John 12:16, 23, 28; 13:31ff; 17:1, 4f.

This lesson also echoes the themes of the previous lesson by once again presenting Jesus as the light of the world (John 11:9-10). Clearly, Jesus is the light of the world, and by Jesus' light men walk safely, apart from him, men walk in darkness and stumble repeatedly.

The Action

In The Story

The lesson for this Sunday is the pivot point of the Gospel of John, as well as for the Lenten season. This is the transition from the public ministry, which concludes with this incident, and the beginning of the Passion Narrative with the triumphal entry into Jerusalem which occupies our attention next week. In many ways, the Lenten season can be best understood as a journey to the cross. This episode is the point at which the focus changes from a public ministry centered on bringing people to faith to the passion which centers on the glorification of Jesus. This story includes references in both directions, to the events which have come before (in addition to those previously mentioned, see also John 11:38), and to events which are coming in the remainder of the gospel.

A common occurrence in John's Gospel, often used as a means to elucidate the action, is confusion on the part of other participants in the action which allows Jesus to explain events. This Johannine confusion occurs at least twice in this story, among the disciples when the news of Lazarus' illness arrives (John 11:8 and 12), and again during the conversation with Martha (John 11:21-22 and 24).

After Jesus clarifies the situation, Martha's response is that of faith incarnate. Significantly, she also uses eschatological titles for Jesus, which is a clear sign that the end is fast approaching.

Finally, this lesson stops much more abruptly than John does. Following the conclusion used here, events in the gospel lead immediately to a description of the plot to kill Jesus. In response, Jesus withdraws to Ephraim (11:54-55) until the Passover crowds began arriving in Jerusalem and provide some safety with the threat of riots if he was captured publicly.

Martha's open confession (John 11:27) can also be considered as part of the reason for the plot to kill Jesus. She provides a rationale for the concern of the Jews which leads them to plot the death of Jesus. Her confession can be taken as evidence that the devotion to Jesus is spreading and taking on political overtones. This is certainly a rationale for Caiaphas' comment in John 11:50 and quite likely one of the things which lead to the comment.

In The Hearers

In this lesson Martha, the faithful follower, comes to a full understanding of Jesus. She begins with faith, but also with a flawed understanding. As a direct result of her conversation with Jesus, she is led to a more complete understanding. This is an endorsement of both the need for faith and the need to strive for a fuller understanding of the meaning of the faith. Some of the Jews who have come from Jerusalem to commiserate with Martha and Mary come to believe as well. Mary, on the other hand, has taken the first steps of faith, but shows no evidence of growth.

Other Jews, starting in John 11:46, plot the death of Jesus. It is an interesting point that verse 46 starts with a "but," as in many conversations. Consider the young woman responding to the offer of a date with "You're nice, but ..." People usually dislike hearing whatever it is that comes after the "but," to the point that merely hearing the "but" is enough to cause a reaction even if the words to follow are not spoken. Here the lessons leave it out, but the results come back in the events we remember over the next two weeks.

If we assume, as seems possible, that Lazarus, Mary, and Martha were prominent citizens of Bethany, it is further reasonable to assume the Jewish leadership in Jerusalem, including Caiaphas the high priest, heard of the events surrounding Lazarus' death and restoration to life quickly, probably from some of the mourners who did not believe in Jesus as a result of these events.

The Sermon

Illustrations

Three quotations about death and immortality:

Maria von Trapp, after the death of her husband, "For hours I would just sit near his grave, begging his pardon and forgiveness. Gladly I would have dug him out with my own hands if I could have made him alive again, giving me another chance."

Publius Syrus, "Grief diminishes when it has nothing to grow upon."

Woody Allen, "I don't want to achieve immortality through my work, I want to achieve it through not dying."

Considering Jesus' maddening delay and the need for patience:

An American tourist couple was eating in a swank Parisian restaurant and the husband was fuming at the delay in getting a waiter to his table. Finally, he yelled, "Hey, waiter. Can't we get any service in this place?"

A waiter appeared and asked frostily, "What would you care to have?"

"Well," drawled the husband, "let's start with a bottle of your best champagne."

"Certainly, monsieur. What year?"

"What do you mean, what year?" screamed the red-faced husband. "Right now!"

When considering the way faith works, for Martha, Mary, and us:

There was a city dweller who retired and bought a small farm and a single cow. A few weeks later the cow went dry. When the newcomer reported this to a neighbor, the neighbor was surprised. The city man said he was surprised as well. "I can't understand it either," he said. "No one was ever as considerate of an animal as I was of that animal. If I didn't need any milk, I didn't milk her. If I only needed a quart, I only took a quart. I just don't understand it."

Of course, a cow must be milked regularly to maintain the flow of milk. And a Christian's faith must be used regularly as a guide for Christian living, not just in times of trial or testing.

Jesus' prayer in John 11:41-42 brings to mind the following story:

A father watched his son carry a heavy rock across the yard. He called out, "Son, why don't you use all your resources?"

The son protested, "But, Dad, I already am!"

"You haven't asked me to help you."

On the need to grow in faith, knowledge, and understanding:

Ed Wynn once commented that he got his first job based on the results of a simple test. Two personnel experts looked into his ears. He was hired, Wynn recalled, "because they could not see each other."

Approaches To Preaching

For those with access to the hymn, "I Receive The Living God" is a recounting of four *ego emi* sayings, including that found in 11:25. Reviewing these sayings as they are presented in the hymn could provide an interesting way to summarize the revelation of Jesus as the Christ and as a summary of the Lenten season as the Sunday of the Passion and Easter approach.

Although there are an abundance of possibilities within the lesson itself, the word which follows this lesson is, in itself, worth at least a mention as a possibility. That word is *but* (John 11:46). Actually a word people dislike hearing, here it certainly changes

66

the significance of the story that forms today's lesson from the climax of the series of miracles which began back in Cana to a proximate cause of the crucifixion. Sermonically, that "but" is a the point of transition for us in this Lenten season, from what we have heard to this point to what we will hear in the next two weeks; public ministry to Passion Narrative.

It is very possible to focus on Lazarus and the way that he has been given a new life. In fact, so have we, in our Baptism. While we haven't had so dramatic a demonstration of this new life as Lazarus did, it is just as real, and should be just as life-changing an event as this likely was for Lazarus. We know little about the remainder of Lazarus' life, but we will know quite a lot about the rest of ours before it is finished. The challenge is to live that new life in faith.

The words of Thomas can form the basis for our answer to that challenge, and as a plan for a Christian life — both for baptismal candidates and for Christians already in the family.

Quite often the stories in the Bible seem somewhat out of touch with the reality that confronts people every day. In the story of the raising of Lazarus, that brutal, dirty reality intrudes in the form of the stench Martha is concerned about. Not that it is merely the smell of death, but a smell that is, after four days, no longer able to be hidden by the oils and spices used in funeral preparations. It seems that no embalming was used in the funerary practices of the time, and any stench was greatly offensive. In fact, in the culture any contact with a dead body was regarded as rendering a person ritually unclean until they had gone through the proper rituals to remove the stain.

The reality of our lives also intrudes and stands in the way of our following Jesus, of doing what he commands us. Sometimes it is a stench we are trying to avoid, other times it is something less offensive, but equally compelling that we wish to avoid (or accomplish) that gets in our way. The real world intrudes in our discipleship quite regularly, and as our Lenten journey draws to a close, it is appropriate to reflect on the ways we fall short because of those intrusions.

Miracle Four

Resurrection

The Text

Early on the first day of the week, while it was still dark, Mary Magdalene came to the tomb and saw that the stone had been removed from the tomb. So she ran and went to Simon Peter and the other disciple, the one whom Jesus loved, and said to them, "They have taken the Lord out of the tomb, and we do not know where they have laid him." Then Peter and the other disciple set out and went toward the tomb. The two were running together, but the other disciple outran Peter and reached the tomb first. He bent down to look in and saw the linen wrappings lying there, but he did not go in. Then Simon Peter came, following him, and went into the tomb. He saw the linen wrappings lying there, and the cloth that had been on Jesus' head, not lying with the linen wrappings but rolled up in a place by itself. Then the other disciple, who reached the tomb first, also went in, and he saw and believed; for as yet they did not understand the scripture, that he must rise from the dead. Then the disciples returned to their homes.

But Mary stood weeping outside the tomb. As she wept, she bent over to look into the tomb; and she saw two angels in white, sitting where the body of Jesus had been lying, one at the head and the other at the feet. They said to her, "Woman, why are you weeping?" She said to them, "They have taken away my Lord, and I do not know where they have laid him." When she said this, she turned around and saw Jesus standing there, but she did not know it was Jesus. Jesus said to her,

69

"Woman, why are you weeping? Whom are you looking for?" Supposing him to be the gardener, she said to him, "Sir, if you have carried him away, tell me where you have laid him, and I will take him away." Jesus said to her, "Mary!" She turned and said to him in Hebrew, "Rabbouni!" (which means Teacher). Jesus said to her, "Do not hold on to me, because I have not yet ascended to the Father. But go to my brothers and say to them, 'I am ascending to my Father and your Father, to my God and your God.' " Mary Magdalene went and announced to the disciples, "I have seen the Lord"; and she told them that he had said these things to her.

Modern celebrations of Easter, particularly in the United States, have actually changed substantially from what was common up to the time of the Civil War (1861-1865). Prior to that time, Easter was observed primarily among the liturgical traditions (Lutheran, Episcopal, and Roman) and generally ignored otherwise. In large part this was due to the influence of the Puritans and their objections to both Christmas and Easter. During the Civil War many churches began to mark Easter as a way to commemorate the dead from the war.

Today there is very little remembrance of the Civil War dead on this day, and much more of a focus on the original events of the day. The lesson for this day completes the Johannine plan begun three weeks ago with the healing of the man born blind, continuing through the raising of Lazarus, the entry into Jerusalem, the events of Holy Week, and finally culminating with the story of the discovery of the empty tomb.

The celebration of the day, which truly stands as the absolute beginning of the Christian church, begins in confusion and misunderstanding. What is now so clear, was at the time quite murky and obscure to those who participated in the events. It can be difficult to recapture this sense, as it is difficult to recapture the exhilaration of Mary and the disciples when they finally realized what had happened. Nonetheless, the effort to understand the range of emotions and to share them as best we can is rewarded by deepening our understanding of the significance of the day.

About The Text

It seems likely that this lesson is the result of the combination of two stories about the events of that morning which have been combined by the author. It should not be a surprise that everyone who had any part in the events would remember them as an important moment in their lives. Two of these reminiscences which present slightly different perspectives seem to have formed the narrative of the lesson for today.

Johannine themes emerge, but the situation is difficult. The Beloved Disciple enters the tomb, sees and believes (20:8), but does not understand what is happening. This is, at best, a curious way to present belief, particularly after the greatest of all signs. At the conclusion of this Gospel Lesson, however, John presents the incident of Thomas and his doubts in 20:19-29, concluding with the summation of the importance of belief in 20:29. This is next week's gospel, which continues the Johannine sequence.

Words

early — Use of this term implies that the gospel is using the Roman ordering system for counting the time. The Jewish started at sundown Saturday, so *early* on the day would have been early evening. It seems that John has an earlier time in mind than the synoptics, which all seem to place the time at some point around dawn (Mark 16:2; Matthew 28:1; and Luke 24:1). John specifically states that it was still dark when Mary Magdalene arrived at the tomb. This could be a matter of only a few minutes, or perhaps a longer time.

the first day of the week — This is the way all the gospels identify the day on which the resurrection took place. This is a designation which reflects mundane matters of dating, not theology, and is carried through even to the book of Peter. A theological dating of the events would follow the formulation of Luke 24:21 and 46 — "on the third day" (see also, aside from the predictions of the synoptics, Acts 10:40 and 1 Corinthians 15:4).

This use of the common method of identifying a day of the week serves to reinforce the idea that not only did the resurrection

71

occur as business was resuming in Jerusalem (the first century equivalent of Monday morning), but also that the stories seem quite likely to go back to eyewitness recollections that used normal, common dating methods rather than theological constructs.

came to the tomb — It is not at all clear why Mary came to the tomb. The synoptics say she was there (with other women) to anoint the body (Mark 16:1; Luke 24:1), while Matthew seems to have dealt with that need before the burial, as well as providing for Mary Magdalene and the other Mary to observe the tomb (Matthew 27:59-61). In this text, Mary simply goes to the tomb, with no reason offered for the trip. John seems to imply she came to weep and wail, i.e. mourn the dead (as the Jews had done for Lazarus in 11:31).

So — This word introduces a point of difficult logic. In Greek, the word translated here is often used to indicate that what follows is a logical outgrowth of what has just been mentioned. Here it is unclear exactly why Mary would run to Peter and the other disciple. It is possible that the text implies Mary looked into the tomb and discovered it was empty or, alternatively, that the stone being moved was enough to indicate the tomb was empty.

An alternate translation is that the word is used to indicate the continuation of a previously interrupted narrative, but that is difficult to demonstrate here. The best suggestion is that the word was a part of the source John used, and was not changed even though the word interrupts the logical flow. It is possible that 20:2-10 is taken from a separate source, and originally 20:11 followed immediately after 20:1. This would produce a much more logical flow of events.

Simon Peter — The generally recognized leader of the disciples is Simon Peter, but in much of the Gospel of John other disciples are equally prominent. Two weeks ago, for example, Thomas was highlighted as a leader of the disciples. Again next week, Thomas will be the most prominent among the disciples when he demands to see Jesus' wounds from the crucifixion. It is possible that in this instance Simon Peter was merely the most convenient of the disciples. In John 16:32, Jesus prophesies that the disciples will be scattered, each to his own home. It is sometimes suggested that Peter was staying in the home of the other disciple, who is generally known as the Beloved Disciple. This would explain why both the disciples went running to the tomb and remove the difficulty of assuming Mary ran to two separate homes to repeat her breathless news.

As a sidelight to this issue, 20:10 says the disciples returned to their homes, which is a fulfillment of the prophecy of John 16:32. The idea that the disciples actually owned homes in Jerusalem is not consistent with the usual picture of the disciples as working folks, and can easily be interpreted as meaning the places where they were staying, i.e., the homes of believers in Jerusalem which were opened to provide the disciples with places to reside while they were there for the celebration of the Passover. This comment also tends to work against the common image of the disciples in an upper room, seemingly living there in a group for mutual consolation and support.

we do not know — In each of the synoptic accounts, a group of women go to the tomb and discover that it is empty. Mark 16:1 mentions three women, Matthew 28:1 only two, and Luke 24:10 mentions three women by name and insists that there were also others. John only mentions Mary Magdalene (who is mentioned consistently in all accounts), but she then uses the plural pronoun in reporting to the disciples. It is possible that this is a reflection of the presence of other women in the early morning trip to the tomb. The alternative is perhaps an assumption of Mary's use of the "royal we."

outran — It is generally assumed that the Beloved Disciple was younger than Peter during their run to the tomb. A medieval commentator attributes the greater speed to the fact that the Beloved Disciple was unmarried, but offers no particular evidence to demonstrate that point, or why it would necessisarily result in greater speed.

73

bent down — Archaeological work has found many tombs of this era that were dug horizontally into the hillsides. This detail in John's account likely indicates an accurate description of the action necessary to see into a horizontal tombs with a small door.

did not go in — The fact that the Beloved Disciple is reported to wait for Peter to arrive is often cited as proof of Peter's preeminence among the disciples. Other options include the possibility that the Beloved Disciple was afraid, or wished to avoid the possibility of touching a corpse. These options are not consistent with the picture John presents of the Beloved Disciple in this gospel as an idealized follower of Christ.

On the issue of deference, the next phrase is worth considering: It is possible that the presence of the Beloved Disciple is an addition of the evangelist, and this seeming deference is not to Simon Peter but to a strong existing tradition that Simon Peter was the first disciple to enter the empty tomb. Rather than contradict the commonly-known story, John introduced the idea of waiting for Peter to arrive.

followed him — In the Gospel of John the term used in the Greek, and translated here, usually indicates a form of discipleship (see 1:44; 8:12; 10:4 and 27; 12:26; and 21:19, 20, and 22. Possibly 1:37 is also intended as an example of this usage, but this is more doubtful). It is possible that, in order to counteract the implication of the Beloved Disciple's seeming deference, the term is used here to indicate that Peter in fact follows the Beloved Disciple.

he saw and believed — These are very difficult words. The expected result of a sign in John is to cause belief, which seems to occur here. But the belief that is engendered here is a rather odd belief, especially in light of the statement in the next verse that at this time they did not understand the scriptures. While the comment in 20:9 does align rather nicely with the Lucan explanations of the incident on the road to Emmaus (Luke 24:13-35) and at the ascension (Luke 24:44-49), it also makes this into a confusing statement.

74

Further, the belief of the Beloved Disciple is apparently not shared with either Peter or, if she had returned with the disciples, Mary Magdalene. Belief in John generally leads to witnessing to the newly-grasped truth (there is no trace of the Messianic secret of the synoptics in the fourth gospel), but here it results only in a profound silence.

Mary stood — When last seen, Mary was breathlessly telling Peter and the Beloved Disciple about the absence of Jesus' body. Her return to the tomb is not mentioned in the text. The timing of the return might be significant. If she had followed the disciples closely, and was there for most of the action, why hadn't the Beloved Disciple communicated his insight to her? If, on the other hand, Mary was somewhat slower in returning to the tomb, it is possible she arrived only an instant before the disciples left the tomb to return to their homes (20:10).

It seems likely that this is a point at which a separate tradition was joined to the narrative. This could be the original continuation of 20:1, or it could be an additional tradition of a visit by Mary Magdalene to the tomb and her discovery that it was empty.

weeping — The word used in the Greek can mean either the mourning which was to be expected at the tomb, or a more spontaneous effusion of tears. While it has been suggested that Mary's purpose in coming to the tomb was to mourn Jesus' death, at this point she seems to be crying tears of sorrow at finding the body gone, and most likely (at least to her) stolen.

Woman — The term is addressed to Mary Magdalene in both 20:13 and 15. The same term is addressed to Mary, mother of our Lord, in John 2:4 during the story of the wedding at Cana; and to the Canaanite woman in Matthew 15:28. The term is certainly not the most respectful term possible, and, in fact, is often presented as at least mildly derogatory. To some extent, the term is probably to be understood as a usage typical of the time if not particularly politically correct in the early twenty-first century. The use of the term both here and in 2:4 might be taken as a sign of some early confusion over exactly who was at the tomb, more precisely — which Mary or Marys were present?

gardener — While this is a *hapax legomenon* in the New Testament, the word is common in secular *papyri*. It simply means one who tends the garden, which John alone describes as the setting for the tomb (19:41). The question does arise of what the gardener was wearing. A gardener might be expected to wear few clothes, but the graveclothes had been left in the tomb. There is no true indication that Jesus appeared nude, but the source of the clothes he might have been wearing is not clear.

in Hebrew — The term is actually in Aramaic, not Hebrew.

Rabbouni! (which means Teacher) — This is an interesting term. As it appears, it seems to be an affectionate term, a diminutive form, which might be translated as "My dear Teacher." In years to follow, the term was also applied to God in rabbinic literature. The term can also be taken to mean Master (in either an academic or political sense) or Lord.

Do not hold on — This is a rather curious comment. It seems that Mary, impulsively, made an effort to hug Jesus as soon as she recognized him. Is this to be taken as an indication that Jesus' body was no longer fully flesh? The suggestion has been made that the clothing left in the tomb was left as it had been arranged on the body, and then Jesus simply passed through it without changing its relative position. In this circumstance, perhaps his body was not yet fully corporeal. No matter how this comment is understood, it clearly represents some sort of a temporary lack of physical firmness. Soon, Jesus will allow Thomas to place his fingers in his wounds (John 20:27) and will share a breakfast of bread and fish with his disciples (21:9-14), so the condition is clearly temporary.

Another understanding is that the basic relationship between Mary Magdalene and Jesus has changed, and this is a signal that there is no longer a physical component of any sort to it. While this

76

view has met great popularity in a variety of novels and among some commentators, with a particular emphasis on the assumption of an intimate physical relationship prior to the resurrection, such an assumption is not required by this phrase.

Perhaps the least likely possibility is that Mary received a sort of "partial" resurrection appearance. Only later did Jesus make "full" appearances to his disciples and others. This is certainly not implied by the text, and seems more of an effort long after the fact to diminish Mary Magdalene's role in these events (contrary to the clear testimony of all four gospels).

Parallels

The synoptic accounts of the empty tomb embody a number of parallels to the account found in John, but as might be expected, John tells the story in his own particular way. The similarities can be listed as follows:

1. The events took place on the first day of the week.
2. The stone had been removed from the entrance to the tomb.
3. Mary Magdalene went to the tomb (perhaps alone, perhaps with other women).
4. There was an angelic presence at the empty tomb (Mark and Matthew mention only one angel, Luke and John mention two).
5. Those who actually found the empty tomb told the disciples of the discovery.

Based on these similarities, it is apparent that there is a very early agreement on the events of this particular morning. Each evangelist chooses to emphasize other details, as should be expected, to emphasize their particular theological insight into the events.

Matthew and John are the only evangelists to record a meeting with the resurrected Christ at (or near) the tomb. In John's case, this served to strengthen the identification of Jesus with the angels in the tomb (they all asked Mary Magdalene the same question — "Woman, why are you weeping?"), as well as laying the foundation for the ascension as the event when Jesus will attain his full glorification. Thus, in the Gospel of John, the empty tomb is not the climax of the gospel. It serves as both the physical demonstration of the truth of the resurrection and as the next step in the glorification of the Son of Man which began as Jesus was lifted up on the cross.

The book of Peter complicates the picture even more. In that source, the two angels are involved with the guards at the tomb (a detail John never mentions) and in clearing the way for the events of Easter morning. While this is clearly not a detail we need to be concerned with, it does point out the tendency to add further details to the recital of events in the gospel itself. While this is a normal tendency, harmonizing the accounts robs them of the unique theological perspective each has to offer.

The People

In many ways the people involved in these scenes are so familiar that we assume we know about them. This issue is, potentially, compounded by the Revised Common Lectionary, which lists John 20:1-18 as a Gospel Lesson appointed for the Resurrection Of The Lord in all three cycles (with the account from the appropriate synoptic account being listed as an alternative in each appropriate year).

Nonetheless, at least three of the individuals in the account are worth at least a brief review to see the way they participated in these events.

As Individuals

Mary Magdalene's historical title, *apostola apostolorum* (or *apostle* [a feminine form] *to the apostles*) serves as an indication of the importance attached to her in the early years of the Christian church. While modern churches have often forgotten, obscured, or intentionally downplayed the role of at least one woman (according to John), the early church honored her with a title indicating her actions as recounted in this lesson.

It was Mary Magdalene who found the empty tomb, who informed the disciples of that fact, and who first met the risen Christ (according to Matthew and John). It was Mary Magdalene who proclaimed the gospel to the apostles, the ones later known for their proclamation of that same gospel.

In this story Mary began with an incorrect understanding of the significance of the events. It was only after she met the angels in the tomb and the risen Jesus that she understood what had happened. And it is only then that she once again seeks out the disciples and tells them, "I have seen the Lord."

The Beloved Disciple has likely been introduced into this narrative by John to lend credence to the entire gospel, as a document written by an eyewitness to the pivotal events of the story. Even so, his presence does serve to represent the other disciples (whose presence is hinted at in 20:9). It is not unlikely that others among the disciples might have made the trek to the tomb once the fact that it was empty was made known to them. While the question of the location of the body was asked only by Mary (or perhaps by the women with her) in this account, it was certainly a question of great interest to the men as well, at least until Mary came to tell them she had actually seen the Lord.

Simon Peter, his role not highlighted as frequently in this gospel as it is in the synoptics, is certainly highlighted in this lesson. He is the disciple Mary runs to inform of the empty tomb. He is accorded the respect of being the first to enter the empty tomb. Even if he is slow to grasp the significance of the empty tomb (which the Beloved Disciple seems to grasp almost instantaneously when confronted with the tomb itself), Peter is still recognized by the time the Gospel of John was written as a leader of the church and as a first witness to the empty tomb. This is reflected in the Johannine account.

As Images And Signs

To an extent which is not completely clear, it is possible to perceive friction between the Petrine leadership and the leadership of a faction headed by the Beloved Disciple in the early church. Based on John 21:24, this second faction is also able to be called the Johannine faction. While the friction certainly did not explode into a schism, it does help explain many of the differences between

John and the synoptics, which are largely based on Mark, the gospel traditionally based on Peter's memories.

In examining Jesus' response to Mary Magdalene's outburst after he revealed himself to her, most of the emphasis has been on the first phrase — "Do not hold on to me." Theologically, the emphasis should be placed on the second phrase — "I have not yet ascended to the Father." The fourth gospel can be understood as building to the moment of the ascension from the beginning. It is only at that point that Jesus is fully and completely glorified, and at that point that his mission on earth is completed.

The ascension begins when Jesus goes up to Jerusalem on the Sunday of the Passion. Not only is this the traditional way to refer to travel to Jerusalem (which is reflected in John 12:20), it also takes into account the geographical fact that the only way to get to the ancient city is to physically climb up to the elevation on which it is located. Thus, the ascension begins with Jesus' journey to Jerusalem.

The next step is the ascension to the cross. This is the key point at which the glorification of Jesus actually begins. At the point reached in this lesson, the interim between the commencement and the fulfillment of the glorification with Jesus' ascension to the Father, Jesus is still in an interim condition, with the fulfillment to come. This point is emphasized by the use of the present tense in Jesus' statement to Mary Magdalene; he is in the midst of the process of ascending at that moment. In point of actual fact, the final fulfillment is not a part of the gospel record in the Johannine tradition. We must remember that, apparently, ascension does not mean that Jesus has departed completely and forever from this world, as there are further resurrection appearances to be made.

The Action

In The Story

The details of the action of the story make it sound inherently believable, even though what is described is inherently unbelievable. Setting out for the tomb in the dark, and finding a stone that is

80

mysteriously removed, set the stage for a dramatic revelation, which Mary Magdalene makes when she announces to Simon Peter and the Beloved Disciple that Jesus' body is missing.

Peter and the disciple, ignoring the question of how they knew the location of the tomb, rush to the tomb with Peter lagging behind the Beloved Disciple. It is expected that two people running to a distant goal will arrive at different times. The Beloved Disciple arrives first, but does no more than look into the tomb. The text says he bent over to look, as would be expected for a tomb with a low entrance, not to mention that someone who has been running might bend over to regain his breath. In the early morning light he saw wrappings laying where the body had been, but the body was clearly gone.

Then he waited for Peter to arrive. When Peter came to the tomb he entered it, followed by the Beloved Disciple. The wrappings of the body were lying there, apparently where the body had been laid. The general assumption is that the body had been laid on a shelf, which was a typical arrangement. For what it might be worth, after about a year, when the body had disintegrated, the bones remaining would be gathered up and placed in an ossuary (bone box), such as those that have been found recently bearing the names of Caiaphas and James.

After checking out what was to be seen, the two disciples left and returned to their homes. This can be understood as both a true detail and a fulfillment of Jesus' prophecy in 16:32. The comment about the Beloved Disciple's belief notwithstanding, Peter and the Beloved Disciple did not understand what had happened well enough to communicate anything of significance after their examination of the empty tomb.

Mary Magdalene is the first character in the story to gain an understanding of the events in anything like a complete, verifiable way. This is not due to any overwhelming intelligence on her part, but because she has the events explained to her. She then shares her information with the disciples. This is the detail which, consistently among the gospels, strikes the chord of accuracy most clearly. In general, people seem to prefer to ignore facts which are embarrassing to them. The Bible is generally noted for including such facts, as seems to be the case here. Thus Peter and the Beloved Disciple, two leaders of the church, are shown as not being able to understand the foundational event of the church. They must have the significance of the events explained to them by a woman.

It is quite likely this represents a highly accurate memory, since a woman who functions as the first proclaimer of the good news is not what would be expected.

In The Hearers

In fact, a quick review of the subsequent treatment of Mary Magdalene indicates how unpopular it has been to recognize her role as the first proclaimer. In some traditions her contribution to the action has been either ignored or relegated to midweek lessons (as opposed to the gospel appointed for a Sunday). It is quite possible to show a number of instances in which Mary Magdalene has been denigrated and consigned to the back room rather than the center of the stage where this lesson places her.

The details make the inherently incredible story credible — the details of the location of the grave clothes and the separate placement of the cloth from Jesus' head, Mary's announcement to the disciples of the significance of the events, and so on. In general, the story is in line with the other signs of the fourth gospel, designed to bring people to faith. In this case, it is not the people in the story who are being brought to faith, it is those who hear the story who are meant to be brought to faith.

The Sermon

Illustrations

This is, after all, Easter Sunday. It is likely appropriate to notice Easter eggs on this day. They derive from pagan sources, both Egypt and Persia, among others, where they were fertility symbols. Among Christians, Easter eggs are often said to be symbols of the tomb. The color red has traditionally been a favorite color for eggs among Christians. This brings up the possibility of a children's sermon using both a blown egg and a raw egg. After discussing Easter eggs, crack the raw egg into a bowl and comment on the problem of an uncooked Easter egg. Then, holding the blown egg over the palm of a hand, smash it with the other hand. The dramatic point is the surprise of the empty egg, just as Peter, and Mary Magdalene, and the Beloved Disciple were surprised by the empty tomb.

At a chapel of early Christians excavated at Dura Europa and dated to the 230s, the main scene on the north wall is three women moving toward a yellowish-white sarcophagus. They are holding torches and dressed in graceful *pallae* — the formal garments favored by established families. The scene is significant as a testimony to the place of honor given in the early church to Mary Magdalene as the *apostola apostolorum*, for she is one of the women carrying torches as they enter the garden before dawn seeking the tomb of Jesus. This early painting is a good example of an emphasis on Mary's witness as proof of the truth of the resurrection.

A comment on the disciples' lack of understanding, and our similar shortcomings:

A mother once spoke sharply to her daughter, "Brittany! Why are all those ants coming out of your closet?"

"They must be coming out of my hope chest."

"Hope chest?"

"Yeah. I've been saving sugar cubes for the day when I get a horse."

We celebrate Easter each year. Does it ever resemble astronomy?

A world famous astronomer once sat next to a fifteen-year-old girl at a dinner. She asked him what he did, and he replied that he studied astronomy. She sniffed slightly and told him, "Oh, I finished that course last year."

The inability of the disciples to understand what had happened is rather like dialing a wrong number:

A strange voice on the telephone said, "Come on over, we're waiting for you."

Annoyed at the interruption, the response came back, "To whom do you wish to speak?"

After a long pause came the response, "I'm sorry. I must have a wrong number. Nobody I know says 'whom.'"

Approaches To Preaching

Picking up the question of two weeks ago, regarding the location of Lazarus' body, three times in this lesson the body of Jesus is missing and asked for (20:2, 13, and 15). Even after an annual celebration of Easter, the events of the day still have the ability to surprise us. This repeated question can be used in a number of ways — as a reminder of the way we search for things we really have no need for, "Where did you hide the body?"; as an entry into the surprise of this day, "Where is the body?"; or even as a straight question, "Where is Jesus?"

These events all took place on the first day of the week, the first century equivalent of a Monday morning. For most people it was business as usual, with about as much complaining about returning to work as can be heard on an average Monday morning in many offices. Then there were the disciples and Mary Magdalene, for whom the day began with business as unusual, about as unusual as it could ever be.

The lesson today includes stories which likely come from the memories of Mary Magdalene and Peter (and, perhaps, the Beloved Disciple). Consider questions like, "Where were you when you heard about ... Challenger, JFK, Pearl Harbor, 9/11?" In the first century, the question would have been where were you on that morning? Somehow Easter isn't nearly as important an event for us as it was for them.

Miracle Five

Ascension

The Text

*Then he said to them, "These are my words that I spoke
to you while I was still with you — that everything written about me in the law of Moses, the prophets, and the
psalms must be fulfilled." Then he opened their minds
to understand the scriptures, and he said to them, "Thus
it is written, that the Messiah is to suffer and to rise
from the dead on the third day, and that repentance
and forgiveness of sins is to be proclaimed in his name
to all nations, beginning from Jerusalem. You are witnesses of these things. And see, I am sending upon you
what my Father promised; so stay here in the city until
you have been clothed with power from on high."*

*Then he led them out as far as Bethany, and, lift-
ing up his hands, he blessed them. While he was blessing them, he withdrew from them and was carried up
into heaven. And they worshiped him, and returned to
Jerusalem with great joy; and they were continually in
the temple blessing God.*

*In the first book, Theophilus, I wrote about all that Jesus
did and taught from the beginning until the day when
he was taken up to heaven, after giving instructions
through the Holy Spirit to the apostles whom he had
chosen. After his suffering he presented himself alive
to them by many convincing proofs, appearing to them
during forty days and speaking about the kingdom of
God. While staying with them, he ordered them not to
leave Jerusalem, but to wait there for the promise of*

85

*the Father. "This," he said, "is what you have heard
from me; for John baptized with water, but you will be
baptized with the Holy Spirit not many days from now."*

*So when they had come together, they asked him,
"Lord, is this the time when you will restore the kingdom to Israel?" He replied, "It is not for you to know
the times or periods that the Father has set by his own
authority. But you will receive power when the Holy
Spirit has come upon you; and you will be my witnesses
in Jerusalem, in all Judea and Samaria, and to the ends
of the earth." When he had said this, as they were watch-
ing he was lifted up, and a cloud took him out of their
sight. While he was going and they were gazing up toward heaven, suddenly two men in white robes stood
by them. They said, "Men of Galilee, why do you stand
looking up toward heaven? This Jesus, who has been
taken up from you into heaven will come in the same
way as you saw him go into heaven."*

The Ascension Of The Lord, which comes forty days after Easter according to both Acts 1:3 and the liturgical calendar (which derives from Acts in this case), is always on a Thursday. For this reason
it is not observed in many congregations, and even when observed,
attendance at Ascension worship services is often rather sparse. For
this reason, it seems, the lection appointed for this day is identical in
each of the three cycles in the church year. The First Lesson in all
cases is Acts 1:1-11, and the Gospel Lesson is Luke 24:44-53.

Luke very carefully divides his two volumes (Luke and Acts)
at the event of the ascension, with the gospel coming first, and the
history of the church coming second. Unfortunately, the requirements of the traditional worship and the order in which readings
are presented means that the readings are presented in the opposite
order. While this is not a plea for scrapping the traditional order of
readings, it is offered as a possible rationale for reversing the traditional order on this day.

These readings include Luke's transition between the gospel
and the history, namely Acts 1:1-5. This transition begins with a
summary of the gospel, and particularly of the resurrection, which
was the most important event of the first volume. Many of the

themes from the first volume are to be fulfilled and expanded in this second volume. In many ways this is accomplished by this transition which also serves to make the entire book of Acts a fulfillment of the work of Jesus.

About The Text

The two lessons, presented here in the order in which they were first presented by Luke, have been challenged by some commentators as not truly belonging to the text of the Lucan narrative. The arguments revolve largely around the particular word choices made in these sections. With words not commonly found in the Lucan vocabulary, some have opted to suggest these verses do not belong in the original, but were added later to the text. Closer examination does reveal some vocabulary differences, but the theology and style of these sections make the vocabulary issues less than decisive.

In fact, by insisting that the ascension is the point of transition between the two portions of his narrative, Luke manages to construct a rather dramatic end to the gospel and a dramatic beginning to the history. While there are some difficulties between the two accounts, in general, the history expands the description of events found in the gospel.

Words Of Luke 24:44-53

I was still with you — This incident takes place after the resurrection, and the relationship between Jesus and his disciples has changed. Rather than being incarnate, Jesus is now in a resurrected body, and soon to be physically gone. Already, the relationship has changed, a fact which is reflected in this introduction.

Moses, the prophets, and the psalms — This reflects the traditional Hebrew division of the scriptures. While the Hebrew Scriptures as a whole are referred to a number of times, this is the only use of this structural reference in the New Testament. Taken in conjunction with other references, particularly those ascribed to Jesus, it is clear that he was well versed in the Hebrew Scriptures, and had a knowledge of them which was based in that tradition.

opened their minds — This reference to opening the disciples' minds is a clear parallel to the episode earlier on the road to Emmaus (Luke 24:13-35). In both instances, insight into events comes from interaction with the resurrected Christ, who opens the scriptures (on the road to Emmaus) or the disciples' minds to understand the scriptures (in this episode). Further, the details of the resulting understanding are similar as well.

witnesses — The word used here for witness derives from the law courts, and is also found in Acts. The concept of basing this gospel on the testimony of witnesses is very important for Luke, as he could not claim to have been an eyewitness himself. Since he is writing a derivative work connecting his gospel to the testimony of eye witnesses lends it an additional cachet of veracity which is quite important.

beginning from Jerusalem — Luke uses a theological construct to frame the growth of the church which he is going to report in the next half of his work. This phrase is the first portion of that construct, and here the grammar involved is ambiguous enough to allow the phrase to be connected to either the preceding or following phrases. The NRSV, and most other translations, place the phrase with what precedes it, as in the text of the NRSV. The possibility must be allowed for that the text really belongs with what follows, as in the NRSV footnote. The meaning is slightly different with the second option, which connects the Jerusalem beginning with the eyewitness basis of the proclamation.

my Father — Luke includes a number of echoes to the Gospel of John, in this case to John 15:16. The promised gift from the Father leads directly to the story of Pentecost in Acts, which is another connection from this story to another writing.

stay here — Clearly the city where the disciples were to stay has rather elastic boundaries, since in the next verse Jesus leads them to Bethany. There are two possible explanations for this anomaly.

First, Bethany was regarded as close enough to Jerusalem to allow people staying there during Passover to participate in the activities in the temple. Clearly this is what Jesus and his companions had done in the past, so it is not beyond the realm of possibility that the disciples continued the practice after the ascension and still regard themselves as following Jesus' instructions.

Second, Jesus' instructions only applied after he ascended. Until that time he led the disciples where he pleased, including the familiar ground of Bethany.

It should also be noted that Luke includes this instruction even though it seems to contradict the evidence of Mark 16:7 (and the parallel in Matthew 28:7) about an Easer morning instruction to go to Galilee, and the reports in Matthew 28:16 and John 21:1 that the disciples met Jesus in Galilee. Luke is clearly writing from a theological perspective that enables him to disregard historical reports and evidence contrary to his theological understanding.

Bethany — The small town of Bethany seems to have been the usual place for Jesus and his disciples to stay during Passover. As a result of this, it seems logical that this location was also well supplied with followers of Jesus (according to John 11:1, Mary, Martha, and Lazarus lived here, and the donkey he rode on Palm Sunday was also provided by a follower from here according to Mark 11:1), which made his stays there relatively safe. In Mark 11:11-12 (and the parallels in Matthew 21:17; Luke 19:29; and John 12:1) Jesus is staying in Bethany while he is actually visiting Jerusalem and worshiping in the temple. Jesus also was invited to dinner during his stays in Bethany (Matthew 26:6). New Testament references to this town near Jerusalem (eleven of them), locate the village on the slopes of the Mount of Olives, which places the ascension in a mountainous locale.

lifting up his hands — The last image of Jesus in Luke's Gospel finds him in a priestly stance, a pose of benediction. This represents yet another link to John, where Jesus also appears in a priestly role when he delivers what is known as the high priestly prayer (John 17).

carried up — The Gospel of Luke ends with the impression that the ascension happened quite late on Easter evening. Acts begins by correcting, or updating the impression. Some of the manuscripts omit this phrase, and scholarly opinion seems somewhat divided on its inclusion.

The debate seems to focus on this word. For Luke the ascension is the glorification of Christ, which comes only after the resurrection (in a point of theological differentiation, John's glorification begins when Jesus is raised up on the cross). The word used here in Greek is also the word used for the action of the priests in the temple in elevating the sacrifices of the people. Thus, the earthly Jesus is, in his final scene on earth, raised up as the ultimate sacrifice, a theological point similar to that made later in the book of Hebrews.

Some commentators feel this word is not emphasized here, and suggest that this omission of emphasis represents the original text. Others suggest that the phrase is omitted to make the end of Luke fit better with the beginning of Acts. It is likely that the latter position is the more rational, but the evidence for either position is not completely conclusive.

in the temple — It must be remembered that the Gospel of Luke ends at a time long before the Christians' breach with the Jews, when worship in the temple was still regarded as the proper behavior for a Christian with a Jewish background (which was pretty much everyone who was a Christian at the time of the end of the gospel). Historically, Christians would spend forty to fifty years following the ascension faithfully worshiping in the temple. It was only with the destruction of the temple by the Romans in 70 C.E. that Christians in Jerusalem ended their worship in the Temple.

Words Of Acts 1:1-11
all — This word betrays a desire on Luke's part to fix the form of the memories of Jesus according to his own theological understanding of the events. Likely this is not an indication of a desire to be completely comprehensive in including everything known (see John 20:30-31, which is likely an accurate reflection of Luke's

principles for inclusion as well as John's), but an indication of Luke's principle of including everything necessary to bring a reader to faith (see Luke 1:3-4). Incidents which were difficult to conciliate with his understanding of events were eliminated without apologies.

to heaven — This phrase is actually not included in the Greek text. It is, however, implied by both the context and the action of the ascension which ends Luke and begins Acts, and is, consequently, regularly supplied by translators.

apostles — This term occurs 38 times in the book of Acts. Only in 14:4 and 16 does it refer to Paul and Barnabas. All other references are to the twelve (or eleven), typically in Jerusalem. Clearly, for Luke, the eleven or twelve (following the election of Matthias as a replacement for Judas, Acts 1:15-26) are the leaders of the church, the ones who lend their title to the first era in the history of the church — the Apostolic Age. The minor fact that Acts focuses on Peter and Paul, with only a passing reference to James, has little to do with the *hagiographic* respect he shows for the eleven or twelve leaders.

during forty days — The phrase is much more ambiguous than it might first appear. It might be understood as "constantly with the apostles" for the period of forty days. Alternatively, it might be taken to mean "appeared many times during" this period to the apostles. This ambiguity is present in the Greek and is retained by the NRSV translation.

While staying with them — This word is a *hapex legomenon*, which leads to the problems encountered in the effort to translate it properly. There are at least three possible translations. The first, *eat with them* (literally *eat salt*) emphasizes the fellowship aspects of the relationship during these forty days. In more modern terms, this is a sort of graduate seminar between a beloved professor and his best students as they prepare to leave school.

A second possible translation is *bring together, camp out with.* Not only does this meaning echo the image of John 1:14, it also emphasizes both the new status of the resurrected Christ (which is an echo of Luke 24:44) and the fact that at this time the apostles were all together with Jesus, a sort of primal church council.

A third possibility is that the word in Greek is actually a misspelling of the word which means *stay with, be with, spend time with.* Leaving aside the issue of possible misspellings in the text, there are several texts that actually have the variant spelling. This understanding would emphasize the intermittent nature of Christ's appearances to the apostles during this period, as opposed to a continual presence among them, which seems to be emphasized in the previous translation possibility.

witnesses — Once again, as in the gospel, Luke uses the concept borrowed from the legal system to describe what the apostles will be doing. The Greek word for witness, *marturia*, is the basis for the English word *martyr.* In many ways, this is a telling comment on the nature of the witness which can be called for from a Christian.

Jerusalem — Again, Luke is imposing his theological construct to structure his presentation of events. Historical evidence indicates that Christianity actually originated in a variety of places such as Joppa, Lydia, Damascus, and likely Galilee. All these places saw the rise of local groups of Christians during the period immediately after the resurrection. The other gospels all seem to either have the disciples back in Galilee for resurrection appearances (Matthew and John) or, at the least, being commanded to return to Galilee (Mark). It is probable that, in a strict historical perspective, after Galilee, the disciples went on to other places to proclaim the good news.

gazing up — This is a common expression in Luke. In fact, twelve of the fourteen times the term appears in the New Testament occur in Luke. The term is used with a sense of extended time, in addition to the obvious action, the term also expresses a relatively lengthy duration of an event. Older translations often used the term *eyes fixed*.

heaven — The Greek used here, *ouranos*, can mean either the dwelling place of God (and by extension, God) or merely the sky. Luke uses the term in both ways in his writings, and here it seems to have both meanings at the same time. On the one hand, Jesus ascends to dwelling place of his father while the apostles are simultaneously looking at the sky.

Parallels

The accounts of the ascension in Luke and Acts are, in many ways, without exact parallels in the gospels. The closest parallel is in the text known as the longer ending of Mark. While Mark 16:19-20, and the rest of the longer ending, has been a part of the gospel since ancient times, it seems clear that they originated from a source other than that which produced the rest of the gospel.

The two verses in question here are clearly about the subject of the ascension, their content betrays the likelihood of a date later than the rest of the Gospel of Mark. In Mark's longer ending, Jesus has just delivered his final teaching to the disciples, and he is rather abruptly "taken up into heaven." There, in fulfillment of a popular psalm (110:1), which was taken as a true Davidic psalm, and a prophecy of the Messiah at the time, Jesus "sat down at the right hand of God."

It is this final action of Jesus, the sitting at the right hand of the Father, which seems to have been added and clearly betrays the later origin of the longer ending. Luke, in the story of Stephen in Acts 7, who, at the moment of his execution, sees Jesus standing at the right hand of God (Acts 7:55-56). The posture, standing in Acts and seated in Mark, would seem to be a possible indication that Luke understood the relationship somewhat differently than did the author of the longer ending. In the Letter to the Hebrews, this image also appears, in 1:3, where Jesus assumes a seat at the right hand of God after the ascension.

Aside from an effort to correctly identify the date of the composition of the longer ending of Mark, there is little in these verses that adds to the Lucan images of the ascension. The location of Jesus in heaven, and also on earth is explicitly stated in these verses, but it is only an explicit statement of what Luke has already introduced.

The Gospels of Matthew and John do not contain explicit mentions of the ascension, but Matthew 28:16 frames the final scene of the gospel by placing the disciples on a mountain (Bethany, in Luke, is on the Mount of Olives) worshiping Jesus. The gospel ends with a final summary of Jesus' teaching, which is a vague echo of Mark (in the teaching only, not in the content of the lesson). There are echoes of the ascension scene in John, but the ascension itself is not reported.

The Gospel of John includes a story of Jesus eating with the disciples during an appearance in Galilee (John 21:4-14). This is an echo of the words in Acts 1:4, even though the location echoes Matthew and, to some extent, Mark. Basically, the ascension is reported most clearly and first in Luke and Acts.

The People

As Individuals

The only person actually mentioned by name in these lessons is Jesus. Rather than simply an individual, at this point Jesus must be taken as two distinct identities. The first is that of the physical body which had recently been resurrected. The precise disposition of this body was an issue with which some in the early church were quite concerned. While modern biblical commentators have not been nearly as fascinated as their forebearers with this issue, at one point it was a significant concern. In fact, some modern novelists have found this subject to work as the basis for their works of fiction, usually with someone discovering the remains of a body which is subsequently identified (or misidentified) as the body of Jesus.

In the early church, the issue was not one of identification of the body, but rather one of the disposition. And the ascension resolved the question rather neatly. The physical, resurrected body of Jesus was taken up into heaven, which accounted quite clearly for the current location of the physical body of Jesus.

The other issue involved with Christ involves the promises of presence and support that are made. The clearest promise is, of course, found in the concluding verse of the Gospel of Matthew, also known as the Great Commission. There Jesus says, "And remember, I am with you always, to the end of the age" (Matthew 28:20b).

In Luke, the promise is generally that of baptism with the Holy Spirit within a few days (Acts 1:5). However, the Spirit of Jesus is still a motivating force in the church as it grows in Acts. While the physical body has gone to heaven, the Spirit of Christ remains among the apostles, providing the strength, courage, and wisdom which are needed in the early years of the church.

In Acts 1:10, two men suddenly appear next to Jesus. This mention of two figures has led some to suspect that the incident known as the Transfiguration (Mark 9:2-8; Matthew 17:1-8; and Luke 9:28-36) is actually a resurrection story, if not a reference to the ascension. If, in fact, the ascension is the basis for a misplaced resurrection/ascension account, it is these two men who provide the connective link.

Even without considering the Transfiguration, the comment the two figures make to the apostles in Acts 1:11, "Men of Galilee," might cause some consideration of the witness of the other three gospels, which all include a return by the disciples to Galilee (or an instruction to return in Mark) after the resurrection. It also serves as a reminder that Luke maintains the presence in Jerusalem for theological reasons.

The apostles are, in a way, undergoing a transition parallel to the change from one volume of the Lucan narrative to another, and even, in some senses, parallel to the transition of Jesus from earth to heaven.

It has been said that in the gospels the disciples seem rather slow, frequently asking for explanations of events and often misunderstanding what has been said or done. This pattern continues in Acts 1:6, when the disciples looked to Jesus to restore Israel's political fortunes. However, within a few verses (by Acts 1:14 and

15-17) the disciples are fervently religious, praying together, and then recognizing the need to replace Judas as the twelfth apostle.

After this event, while the apostles are certainly not perfect paragons of wisdom and strength, they change dramatically from the individuals of the gospel. Now they preach without fear, proclaim the good news, and challenge the established authorities. In some ways this dramatic change is a reflection of the presentation by the author. But in some other, quite significant ways this change is best understood as a reflection of the impact of the Spirit of Christ in their lives.

As Images And Signs

The event of the ascension can also be understood as an end and a beginning. This event is the end of the Gospel of Luke, as well as the end of the personal, physical relationship with (or, understood in another way, faith in) Jesus. The ascension is also a beginning, the beginning of Acts as well as the beginning of the apostles' inseparable connection with Christ, a friend and trusted companion both on earth and in heaven.

The Action

In The Story

In Acts 1:3, Luke mentions the "many convincing proofs" by which Jesus proved to the disciples he was alive. Perhaps the most convincing is mentioned in the next verse, which can be translated as "while eating with them." Eating is traditionally thought of as something no ghost can possibly do, hence eating proved the resurrected Jesus was not a ghost. This point is made even more explicit in Luke 24:36-43, which recounts a resurrection appearance which has similarities to John's account of Doubting Thomas.

Jesus appears among the disciples, and they are terrified, since they think he is a ghost. Jesus tells the disciples to look at his hands and feet, and then to touch him, to prove he is not a ghost. When the disciples still seem to have doubts, Jesus provides the ultimate proof of his physical body by taking a piece of boiled fish and eating it in front of them. Similar incidents which involve eating can be found in Mark 16:14 and John 21:12-13. John's recounting of the incident of breakfast at the seaside is heavily overlaid with eucharistic images, but the same can be said for the other references, including the story of the road to Emmaus (Luke 24:30). The common theme among all these stories is the idea that Jesus became known to his followers during the "breaking of bread," or during the sharing of a meal.

The story of the ascension contains a number of difficulties in reconciling the events listed in Luke with the parallel account in Acts. This does not mean that Luke forgot the details, or changed the story between the two accounts. Rather, it is an indication that Luke is writing a theological document, not an unbiased history.

In the gospel, the end of the earthly ministry comes with Jesus taking his leave at the end of the first Easter, with a gesture of benediction borrowed from the priestly practice of the temple. In Acts, Luke is deeply concerned to ensure there is no indication that the church is the creation of human beings alone, hence the need for a final forty days of instruction from the risen Jesus. Not a human venture, but one guided by the risen Christ through its history. In fact, this is a theme that is quite apparent in Acts, where visions, dreams, the Spirit, and the Lord intervene in the action with some regularity to ensure it progresses properly.

Thus, the story of the ascension serves two different purposes, one in each version in which it is found. Not that new information arrived between the appearance of the gospel and the history, but that the theological nature of the larger story made it necessary for the details to adjust accordingly.

In The Hearers

Those who heard the stories of the ascension likely were not troubled by the variations in the details. Luke, in 1:4 (and supported by John 20:31), indicates his purpose in writing these materials is to convince his hearers (or readers) of the truth of Jesus and his ministry that they might believe in him. The stories of the ascension not only settled the nagging minor question of what happened to the resurrected physical body of Jesus (a question similar

97

to the question of "Who was Mrs. Cain?"), but also emphasized that the actions of the apostles were based firmly on the instruction they had received from the resurrected Christ. Hence, the change from less than astute followers, to fearless, intrepid leaders can be attributed to this period of instruction.

The Sermon

Illustrations

Between Luke and Acts, the picture of the apostles changes dramatically, but change can be a difficult thing to face and endure:

During the early days of World War II the British were hard pressed to find artillery to defend their shores against an anticipated invasion. Manpower was also in short supply, and every source was tapped. Finally, the crew manning a piece of artillery which had, in days gone by, been drawn by horses, was under study. The piece was terribly slow to fire, so a time-motion study expert was brought in to see what could be done to improve the rate of fire. The expert and his crew took movies of the firing of the gun and studied them in slow motion.

Eventually the crew noticed the two members of the crew who stood perfectly still, then came to attention and held that position for at least three seconds before the gun was fired and stayed in that posture until after the gun was fired. No one could figure out why the men were behaving this way, except that it was called for in the directions for firing the gun. Finally, an elderly artillery officer was consulted. After some initial puzzlement, he finally recognized what the two men were doing. "I have it!" he cried. "They are holding the horses."

Speaking of the concept of witnesses and witnessing:

In the movie *Butch Cassidy and the Sundance Kid*, the title characters are trying to escape a posse, after a train robbery. The posse consists of good horsemen who are relentless in their pursuit of the pair. Finally Butch asks Sundance a question, "Who are those guys?"

98

That is exactly how Christians should witness: quietly, relent-lessly, so that all who see them are moved to ask, "Who are those guys?"

A study was once made, and it was concluded that the average person spoke for only ten or eleven minutes a day. The average sentence takes only two and a half seconds to say. We communicate more through our actions than through our words, more with our eyes and facial expressions, hands and shoulders than with our mouths.

The apostles spent, according to Acts, the forty days between Easter and the Ascension being instructed by the risen Christ. Instruction in the church is more often similar to that of a university in this cynical view:
Universities are full of knowledge. After all, the freshmen arrive knowing everything, and the graduating seniors take no knowledge away, so the knowledge must accumulate somewhere on campus.

Approaches To Preaching
As the last illustration points out, the apostles, even after years of traveling with Jesus, and learning from him on a regular basis, spent forty days learning more from him. Even the apostles who had been with him from the beginning, as is clearly the case, based on Acts 1:21-22 underwent this last period of intensive instruction. Clearly there is a need for Christians, even those who have been in the faith for years, to continue to study and learn.

Acts 1:8 serves as the model and pattern for the rest of Acts. This is a typical literary device of Luke, namely to introduce a theme, refer to it again, and only then present it in detail. Thus, as the introduction for the rest of the book this verse sets the pattern which will be followed. The Holy Spirit comes at Pentecost, and then, beginning in Jerusalem and then spreading out to the rest of the world (with the concluding scene in Rome, the center of the known world). This is Luke's theological understanding of the pattern of growth for the church, a pattern he edits the details to present.

99

This is the story of how Jesus, as a physical body, ascended to heaven. The resurrected Jesus returned to heaven. Christ, as a spiritual presence, remains on earth, among his followers until the end of the age, as Matthew expresses it. The two directions in this lesson are pointed out in the two meanings of heaven at the end of Luke.

The two meanings can also be taken as a symptom of this event as both the end (of the gospel) and the beginning (of the history). It can also be taken as the end of our former life and the beginning of our new life in Christ.

The apostles are called, in Acts, to be Christ's witnesses in the world. In *Grandmother and the Priests* Taylor Caldwell has a character remind his listeners that an eyewitness isn't always believed. In fact, eyewitnesses are often doubted, and quite regularly incorrect in their recollections. On the other hand, legends, again based on Caldwell's insight, are often accepted as true largely because they are legends handed down from the past, sanctified by the centuries of repetition they have gone through. By these retellings the stories are lifted above doubt and suspicion.

Miracle Six

Spirit's Coming

The Text

*When the day of Pentecost had come, they were all to-
gether in one place. And suddenly from heaven there
came a sound like the rush of a violent wind, and it
filled the entire house where they were sitting. Divided
tongues, as of fire, appeared among them, and a tongue
rested on each of them. All of them were filled with the
Holy Spirit and began to speak in other languages, as
the Spirit gave them ability.*

*Now there were devout Jews from every nation
under heaven living in Jerusalem. And at this sound
the crowd gathered and was bewildered, because each
one heard them speaking in the native language of each.
Amazed and astonished, they asked, "Are not all these
who are speaking Galileans? And how is it that we hear,
each of us, in our own native language? Parthians,
Medes, Elamites, and residents of Mesopotamia, Judea
and Cappadocia, Pontus and Asia, Phrygia and
Pamphylia, Egypt and the parts of Libya belonging to
Cyrene, and visitors from Rome, both Jews and pros-
elytes, Cretans and Arabs — in our own languages we
hear them speaking about God's deeds of power. All
were amazed and perplexed, saying to one another,
"What does this mean?" But others sneered and said,
"They are filled with new wine."*

*But Peter, standing with the eleven, raised his voice
and addressed them, "Men of Judea and all who live in
Jerusalem, let this be known to you, and listen to what*

101

I say. Indeed, these are not drunk, as you suppose, for it is only nine o'clock in the morning. No, this is what was spoken through the prophet Joel: 'In the last days it will be, God declares, that I will pour out my Spirit upon all flesh, and your sons and your daughters shall prophesy, and your young men shall see visions, and your old men shall dream dreams. Even upon my slaves, both men and women, in those days I will pour out my Spirit; and they shall prophesy. And I will show portents in the heavens above and signs on the earth below, blood, and fire, and smoky mist. The sun shall be turned to darkness and the moon to blood, before the coming of the Lord's great and glorious day. Then everyone who calls on the name of the Lord shall be saved.' "

The evidence is that this festival was celebrated from the beginning of the church on the first Pentecost, fifty days after Christ rose from the dead. From Acts 20:16 it appears that Paul observed the feast of Pentecost, perhaps for the traditional symbolism of the Jewish festival, but also, most likely, for the anniversary of the organization of the church.

A variety of customs grew up in celebrations of the day, including the release of doves from the roof (or into the church from the ceiling), dropping balls of fire from the church roof, and scattering roses upon the congregation. Traditionally the canticle *Veni, Creator Spiritus* was included on this day, as were both the blessing of baptismal fonts and a number of baptisms.

In North America, Pentecost came to be known, from the Dutch settlers in New York, as Pinkster. The celebrations of the festival were known as Pinkster frolics. This name is reflected in the name often applied to Capitol Hill in Albany, New York — Pinkster Hill, apparently because the slaves of colonial days (New York was the last northern state to abolish slavery) held riotous festivities there on the Day Of Pentecost.

The origin of the Christian celebration of Pentecost seems to derive entirely from the needs of Luke's theological chronology. After the resurrection, Christ spent the next forty days (Acts 1:3)

102

instructing the apostles, and then ascended into heaven (Acts 1:9). The next festival in the calendar is that of Pentecost, which suited Luke's purpose admirably.

One question which needs to be posited before a detailed look at the text is that of the identification of the actual miracle in this incident. Perhaps the most obvious miracle is the speaking in languages by the Christians of Jerusalem. While this miracle is sometimes misconstrued, it is certainly, at the very least, a miraculous resolution of the chaos introduced at the Tower of Babel.

A second choice is to identify the miracle of the Day Of Pentecost as the giving of the Holy Spirit to the church. The Holy Spirit is certainly not something the early Christians had earned, or qualified for in any way, yet it was poured out liberally on them.

Or, was the miracle here something else? Certainly, a strong possibility is the substantial change in Peter. Less than two months ago, according to Luke's chronology, Peter was so afraid of the consequences that he denied even knowing Jesus (Luke 22:54-62). Now, after witnessing the resurrection, going through forty days of instruction, and receiving the Holy Spirit this morning, Peter stands up in front of a crowd of Jews and proclaims Jesus to the crowd as Lord. This is, at the least, a rather substantial change in Peter's attitude in a remarkably short time.

About The Text

Words

Pentecost — This is actually a Jewish festival (also known as *shavous*), which falls fifty days after the second day of Passover. Leviticus 23:15-21 and Deuteronomy 16:9-12 provide detailed commands instituting this festival (see also Exodus 23:16; 34:22; and Numbers 28:26). The Jewish festival was originally the culmination of the harvest season, but the agricultural significance was gradually replaced by a commemoration of the giving of the Law on Sinai. Rabbinic scholars determined that the festival of Pentecost happened to fall on the same day that Moses received the Law on Mount Sinai, and thus began a celebration for that event on this day.

103

While this feast day is the least commented on in Jewish writings, having no separate tractate in the Talmud (as do other feast days), references are scattered through other writings. The most significant aspect of the festival is the tradition of serving dairy foods for the main festival meal of this day.

Theologically, Pentecost served Luke's purpose well. The church can be understood as the harvest, and in fact this image can be found in Luke 10:2 as well as in some parables in Luke and the other gospels. The harvest significance fits with the Christian Pentecost, as does the idea of a new law, which is given on this day, with the Spirit.

all — Acts 1:15 indicates the Christians before Pentecost numbered about 120, or at least 120, as the reference could have been to a portion of the Christians who believed at that time. The term *all* is ambiguous here. It may mean all the believers at that time, or only all the apostles. The NRSV retains the ambiguity, while TEV opts for the latter meaning.

While the term is ambiguous here, more precise numbers are important in Acts 2:41, which reports that about 3,000 people were baptized and added to the church on Pentecost.

sound — Contrary to expectations fostered by facile representations of the events, the noise is the subject of the verb *filled*. It was the noise which filled the house, not the violent wind. A noise which came suddenly and filled the house is certainly a cause for some concern, if not fright, confusion, and terror. None of these reactions are reported among the Christians, however; even though they are reported among the Jews later in the lesson.

wind — The Greek word used here, *pnoes*, is closely related to *pneumatos* (Spirit) of verse 4. Sometimes these words seem to be used interchangeably, but only rarely when Spirit is used as part of the technical term Holy Spirit, as it is here.

house — The Greek word *oikos* can refer to either a private home, as is usually assumed here, or to the temple. Luke uses *to ieron* to

104

refer to temple at least 22 times, and other than here does not use *house* in that way. It is quite likely he is referring to a private house here, but understanding the reference as meaning the temple would simplify the action of the story.

as of — Illustrations of the events of Pentecost often show the apostles and others with little flames over their heads. Unfortunately, this is not exactly what the text states. Luke is quite clear it was something *like* tongues of fire, not actual tongues of fire.

Further, the Greek indicates the idea here is that the fire flowed and divided itself to touch each person present. The NRSV, with "divided tongues" has a traditional but infelicitous translation which doesn't really convey what the Greek says. A better image might be that of a bright, fire-like ball which appears and seems to flow until each person in the room has been touched by the blazing light.

rested on — A second part of this verse that contradicts the common illustrations is found in this term. Precisely where the fire-like apparition rested is not stated in the Greek, nor are there any implications of location in this term. Consequently, a variety of options as to the location of the tongues of fire can be considered. It is possible the people were individually engulfed by the fire-like apparition, or that it reached out and brushed their chests (to touch the heart) to fulfill the prophecy of Jeremiah 31:33.

filled with — This term brings two concerns. First, it implies that the apostles were empty before this event, which is a dubious understanding. If they were in fact empty, then what was the purpose of the forty days of instruction between the resurrection and the ascension, not to mention the years spent traveling with Jesus before the Passion? Clearly the apostles were not empty until this event. Rather, the filling needs to be considered as a parallel to filling something already partially full.

The other issue here concerns what they were filled with. The text clearly indicates it was the Holy Spirit that filled them. It is important to note, however, the Holy Spirit was equally clearly not the agent of the action. The action here is not that of fulfilling a prayer which begins "Holy Spirit, come fill...." Rather, this is the gift of the Father, which was promised in Luke 24:49 and Acts 1:4, 8, which fills the Christians without the action of the Spirit itself.

speak — The Greek construction here indicates the ability was given successively, not to all those present at once. The languages involved were languages other than those normally spoken. The word in Greek is used by the Septuagint and in classical Greek to indicate solemn or inspired speech, not an ecstatic utterance of an unknown language. The word appears only in Acts in the New Testament, here, and at 2:14 and 26:25.

every nation — This is not intended as an absolute statement, but as a bit of mild hyperbole. The basic meaning of this phrase is that lots of different places were represented in the crowd which assembled. The list in Acts 2:9-11, the lay reader's nightmare, indicates the diversity of the crowd. This is also meant to be a suggestive, not exhaustive list.

amazed and astonished — In Greek, this is a literary device used to indicate intensity. The crowd was quite bewildered. The image is of a crowd milling around, each person asking their neighbor what is going on.

This term also serves as a clear indication that the languages being spoken were natural (real, commonly known in a particular locale) languages, not ecstatic tongues. The nature of the languages led to the amazement of the crowd that a group of Galileans, who had no way to learn the various languages they were speaking, could actually be speaking this variety of languages so that they could be understood. Speaking in ecstatic tongues, on the other hand, was something even a Galilean was as likely as anyone else to be able to do.

Parthians, Medes ... — The United Bible Societies, in their handbook for those who translate the book of Acts, suggests that no text of Acts should be published without a map indicating where these places are to be found. The suggestion is reasonable, but the map itself presents some difficulties, especially in historical terms. The countries named are generally arranged in east to west, north to south order (but there are some problems, see the next note). They also represent the geographical areas of the Roman Empire which had a reasonably large Jewish minority in residence.

Medes — This term is likely taken from the Old Testament, as this group had long since ceased to exist by the time the book of Acts was written. A similar fate had also overtaken Elam (the home of the Elamites).

from Rome — Most often this term means Roman citizens, not former residents of Rome. It is likely, however, that Luke uses the term in the latter sense here.

standing — This is the posture of a Greek orator, not that of a Jewish teacher (as in Matthew 5:1 and other places). Luke is betraying his Greek orientation, as opposed to the Hebraisms which are more common in the other gospels.

Men of Judea, and all who live in Jerusalem — Peter's speech sounds as if it is addressed to only a small segment of the crowd, which is from every nation. But, it is actually addressed to the entire crowd, which is, for Luke, composed only of Jews. The Jews in the crowd are the Jews from every nation who have come to Jerusalem, most likely to study in the temple with the teachers who held forth there. This is precisely what a Jew from Tarsus named Saul had done. The mission to the Gentiles is not initiated until Acts 10, when Peter baptizes Cornelius, so even with the address which sounds quite inclusive, the speech is actually aimed exclusively to the Jews of Jerusalem.

The fact that the address is to those *who live in Jerusalem* is an indication that the crowd is composed, at least in Luke's mind, of Jews from all over who have taken up residence in Jerusalem, not people in town as visitors for the festival of Pentecost. Even though the festival brought huge crowds back into Jerusalem for a one-day celebration, and some of these people might actually have been in the crowds, theologically it is not appropriate for the newly-baptized members of the church to disperse to the four corners of the earth the day after they join the church.

Thus, Peter's sermon is addressed to the residents of Jerusalem, who have come from all over the empire. These converts can be expected, in all likelihood, to remain in Jerusalem while they learn more about the faith they have just embraced.

drunk — It is an interesting thought to suggest that a drunk becomes intelligible to someone who speaks another language. More often a drunk becomes unintelligible to someone who speaks the same language. Rather than explaining a sudden linguistic facility, the effort of the accusation seems to be to explain the outrageous behavior of a bunch of Galileans who suddenly start shouting in the temple.

nine o'clock in the morning — Obviously, drunks can be drunk this early (either as the residual effect of the evening before, or as the result of an early start on the day), but Peter's point is that morning prayers usually began at this time, and observant Jews, which included the apostles, typically ate only after morning prayers were finished, i.e. usually around ten in the morning.

prophet — The term is used here in the Old Testament sense of God's spokesman, not the more modern understanding as a future seer or fortune teller.

last days — This is a typical Jewish expression indicating the time of the Messianic Age when God would fulfill his promises to his people. These words are not found in either the Greek or Hebrew text of Joel 2:28-32, but are supplied by Peter.

all flesh — This is a messianic sign, the spirit of God is no longer to be largely restricted to the Jews, but to be available to all people.

young men — The term typically indicates those men who are prior to marriage, not only not leaders, but commonly regarded as impetuous and not given to deep thought.

old men — These are respected leaders, trusted counselors, those filling positions typically reserved for elder statesmen.

portents ... and signs — In the New Testament, and often in Acts, this is an idiomatic phrase which functions to intensify the basic meaning of the two words involved — miraculous things. The phrase also occurs in Acts 2:43; 4:30; 5:12; 6:8; 7:36; 14:3; and 15:12. The original text in Joel does not have the intensifying phrase *and signs*.

Lord — At the conclusion of this lesson the term has an ambiguous use. In the Old Testament, Lord is the usual translation for YHWH, the name of God. In Acts, the Greek word is also taken to refer to Jesus. In verse 20, the former meaning is intended; in verse 21, the latter.

Parallels

There are two distinct parallels to this selection from Acts. One set of parallels involves Paul's comments on speaking in tongues, the other is to the portion of Peter's sermon included here which largely comes from Joel.

In 1 Corinthians 14:1-5 Paul speaks of the relative value of speaking in tongues and finds that it is less valuable than the gift of prophecy. Both of these are manifestations of the Spirit, and Paul points out that tongues is the less valuable gift. This point is raised again later in this same chapter. In 14:20-25 Paul begins with a quote from Isaiah 28:11-12 which is fulfilled without reference in the action of this lesson, and uses this quote to demonstrate again that speaking in tongues is a less valuable gift than prophecy. In general, Paul seems to accept speaking in tongues as something that must be put up with, but he consistently emphasizes that other gifts of the Spirit are more valuable in building up the church. Of course, Paul is generally speaking of ecstatic speech, not the image that is presented in Acts.

Paul also quotes Joel 2:32, the final verse of this lesson, in Romans 16:13.

In his sermon, Peter quotes Joel 2:28-32, but with some modifications. Peter adds the opening words and the second half of the phrase *portents ... and signs*, as has already been noted. He also reverses the order of Joel, mentioning *young men* before *old men*, where Joel has the opposite order. Peter also adds *and they shall prophesy*. Even though the changes might seem rather insignificant, in most instances, they do indicate that Peter (or Luke) can easily be understood to be working from his memory of the portion of Joel quoted here, not from a written copy in front of him from which he could copy the words. These sorts of minor modifications seem like precisely the sort of thing which could occur when trying to remember a lengthy quote.

The People

As Individuals

The most prominent individual in this lesson is Peter. In the gospels, Peter is presented as a leader among the disciples, although Thomas fills a similar leadership role in the Gospel of John. In the letters of Paul there is some support for the identification of Peter as a leader in the early church. Certainly there is plenty of evidence to support the view that Peter took a leadership position in the early church. The significant question for scholars is how much of what Acts presents as Peter's role is historically justified? It is certainly possible, perhaps even likely that Peter was the apostle who stood forth and spoke to the crowd, defending the Christians against defamatory charges of drunkenness.

The question might be asked how a relatively unlettered fisherman could begin a sermon by quoting an Old Testament prophet. One supposition is that Peter was actually the product of the synagogue training system, which managed to produce adults who were, at the least, familiar with selected portions of the Hebrew Scriptures. Certainly the citation from Joel would be included in a short list of prophecies concerning the messianic expectations which were rampant during this period, so it might not be too large an assumption to imagine that Peter had memorized the portion of Joel as a

110

part of his synagogue training, which was generally required of boys so that they could become men (through a bar mitzvah).

While Peter was certainly the main character in this lesson, he is not the only character to play an important role. While the other Christians also received the Spirit, Peter is the one who steps forward with the other apostles to speak. In 2:33, the gift of the Holy Spirit clearly included other Christians. It was not limited to apostles, but was a gift given to all the Christians present on the morning of Pentecost.

In writing his materials, one of Luke's favorite literary devices is to identify two opposing groups and then explicate the situation with a dialog between the groups. This is what happens here between the crowd and those in the crowd who thought the apostles were drunk. As happens here, one group, the crowd, is generally well disposed toward Christians, the other group is usually antagonistic to some extent. This device affords Luke the impression of providing a well-rounded picture of events as well as allowing an opportunity and justification for explanatory discourses. This is what happens here, as Peter uses the accusation about new wine as a transition into his sermon.

The crowd as a whole behaves in a way unlike the typical response to a portent or a sign. Rather than believing the good news or in Christ, this crowd simply waits to hear more. While this allows for Peter's sermon, the whole purpose for signs in the gospels and Acts is to instill, engender, and enhance belief, none of which happens here. It is only after the sermon of Peter that over 3,000 people are baptized and come to the church (Acts 2:37-42).

As Images And Signs

In this lesson we have an example of something both basic and significant to the Christian use of the Old Testament. Peter uses an Old Testament prophecy and applies it to the current situation to illuminate what the prophecy actually means. Here he claims further that the events unfolding in front of the crowd's eyes are the prophecy's embodiment and fulfillment.

This approach is actually a vastly different approach than that taken in the Old Testament. There, when a crisis occurred, a new prophet arose and proclaimed the Word of God for the people of God. While often ignored or even actively persecuted (for example, Jeremiah), these prophets eventually gained much respect in Israel for the way they told the people of the Word. For this reason there was little or no re-interpretation of previous prophecies, although Jeremiah ran into troubles when he challenged Isaiah's prophecy about God protecting Jerusalem from foreign invaders. What was true a century earlier was no longer true in Jeremiah's time. Yet, even this change was marked by the presence of a new prophet, not a new interpretation of an existing prophecy.

The New Testament approach is, in general, the reinterpretation of existing prophecies, and their application to the current situation. This approach is not unique to the Christians, as it is also found among the authors of the Dead Sea Scrolls. It is, however, not without its dangers. Without some guidance in the proper manner of reinterpretation, simply looking for some selection from either the Old or New Testament to explicate a current situation can lead to quite disastrous results. The application of biblical prophecies must be done carefully and prayerfully to ensure a reasonable chance of proper application.

The crowd's reaction is mentioned three times in this lesson. They are described as "bewildered ... amazed and astonished ... amazed and perplexed" in various places. These are all typical reactions to God's deeds of power in the New Testament. From reactions to the angels at the time of Jesus' birth to the reactions to the angels at the tomb, fear, bewilderment, astonishment, amazement, and perplexity seem to be the normal reactions. The miracle of tongues aroused these same emotions, but this sign did not lead to the next step which is generally found in the gospels, namely belief or faith (at least in some of the hearers). Belief is supposed to be the result of a sign such as this.

It is possible that this lack is actually a literary device. No faith is engendered from the initial sign, but after Peter explains what is going on, 3,000 come to be baptized and join the church (Acts 2:41). This certainly results in heightening the effect of Peter's sermon, even as it reduces the episode of speaking in tongues to a mere prelude.

This lesson contains three echoes of the Old Testament. First, to Genesis 1:1-2, where a "wind (or Spirit) from God" moves across the waters to initiate creation. In Acts, a noise like a wind and a Holy Spirit from God came to the apostles to initiate a new creation: the church. In Genesis 11:1-9 the story of the Tower of Babel is recounted. There the people were confused by the device of the confusing languages. Here the image is reversed. All the languages are available to those who proclaim the Word of God.

Similarly, in Numbers 11:24-25 the spirit which rests on Moses is shared with the elders who begin to prophesy. The situation is not as clearly echoed in Acts, but the Spirit, symbolized by the tongues as of fire, seems to begin in a central location and then is divided to be shared among the others present. In Acts, the distribution of the Spirit, as in Numbers, also represents a distribution of the leadership role, and a distribution of the ability to prophesy. In Numbers, the prophetic ability is a one-time event, while in Acts the ability is understood to be on-going. Finally, even though Acts presents Peter in a leadership role in the early chapters, and Paul in the latter portions of the work in the same role, the reality of the early church was that leadership was actually quite decentralized. Most of the leadership depended on an individual's ability to convince others to do what was needed, rather than deriving from any offices which had inherent authority. Thus, the distribution of the leadership role is even more widespread in Acts than it was in Numbers.

Finally, the Pentecost of the Jews was originally a harvest festival. The story of the first Christian Pentecost also represents a harvest, this time a harvest of believers for the church. In one day the church grew by more than 2,500 percent. Not only does this rapid growth almost certainly indicate the potential for some problems in assimilation, it also is a sign of the reinterpretation of the festival into an evangelical event.

The Action

In The Story

A very pertinent question regarding this story is to attempt to establish the exact location of these events. As noted, the word *house* could refer to either a private home or the temple. The flow of events would be much more dramatic if the events took place in the temple, but it is most likely that Luke is referring to a private home. The story should not be treated as a description of a documentary film.

There is no mention of any movement from the location of the descent of the Spirit to the location of the speaking in tongues and Peter's sermon. If the Spirit came to the Christians in a private home, there must have been some movement. This also raises questions of the number of people who moved, how many remained in the first location, and even questions of how many people were present in the private home in the first place. A private home that could accommodate 120 Christians (if that is how many people were present) must have been a very large home, even if it is assumed that the home was built on the Roman model with an interior courtyard where the people gathered.

When reading the story we have the disadvantage of familiarity. The noise in Acts 2:1 is not identified as the Holy Spirit until Acts 2:4. Thus, when first heard, the noise is "enigmatic" at the least, perhaps terrifying, and certainly a cause for a case of nerves. Anyone who has lived through a hurricane or tornado, can testify that the sound of a rushing wind is often quite scary. There is a certain implacable nature to the rushing wind, something that is very threatening, even when you are in a well-constructed room or building. Even though not mentioned, it is quite likely that the Christians present were understandably nervous when the sound as of a rushing wind began.

There is also a question of where the understanding of the languages actually did occur. While it is commonly assumed that the speakers were actually speaking tongues which they did not normally speak, it is possible to theorize that the speakers were actually speaking their normal, everyday language, while the listeners *heard* the language they normally spoke. With this understanding, the miracle took place not in the speakers who had been baptized with the power of the Holy Spirit, but in the ears of the listeners who had not.

The idea that what was really involved was not an actual language but ecstatic speech (which is what is found in Numbers and in other places in the New Testament) is not supported by either the plain words of the text or by the Greek which lies behind them. Clearly what the people here were speaking was the normal languages that were familiar to those people listening. Only a true polyglot could manage such a feat without help, and none of the Galileans standing in front of the crowd had attained anything even approaching that level of dexterity of language. In fact, it is possible that the thick Galilean accent might have been quite an impediment to listeners understanding their words even in the Aramaic they commonly used. (The Galilean accent seems to have been behind at least one of the identifications of Peter in Luke 22:54-62.)

A final aspect of the action of the story which might be a source of questions is the matter of why the crowd gathered around the Christians. If, in fact, the Christians were baptized by the Spirit in a private house, then the manifestation of the spirit would likely have been a rather private event, and not likely to draw a crowd. Apparently it was the speech of the apostles which brought forth the crowd, but it is possible to understand Acts 2:6 as reflecting either cause, and the question is submerged in Luke's presentation.

In The Hearers

The action in this lesson is not finished, but continues to the present day. As a result of Peter's sermon, at least according to Luke, the number of believers grew by 3,000 on this day. With very little sign of difficulties, the church continues to grow daily in Jerusalem (Acts 2:46-47). By Acts 5:1-11 there was a misunderstanding that caused problems (Ananias and Sapphira), while Acts 6:1-6 recounts the solution of another problem caused by the rapidly growing church.

While it might be comforting to modern sensibilities to discern the strains of rapid growth in the church in Acts, these incidents can also serve as a reminder that Luke is writing theological history. In other words, what masquerades as history is actually a theologically structured document, with the incidents included generally selected on the basis of the theological impact, not the historical validity of the reporting.

It is reasonable to suspect that at least a few of the 3,000 believers who were baptized on Pentecost might have been tourists in Jerusalem for the festival of Pentecost, returning to their homes throughout the region (or even throughout the whole Roman world) during the next few days. While this is contrary to Lucan theology, it is historically probable, especially in light of the historical growth of the church in other places. Luke does agree that the church slowly begins to spread out from Jerusalem to the ends of the earth, or at least to Rome, where the action of Acts ends.

The Sermon

Illustrations
On the Day Of Pentecost, there is the following idea:

Corrie ten Boom once wrote: "I have a glove in my hand. The glove cannot do anything by itself, but when my hand is in it, it can do many things. True, it is not the glove, but my hand in the glove that acts. We are gloves. It is the Holy Spirit in us who is the hand, who does the job. We have to make room for the hand so that every finger is filled."

Karl Barth once wrote about something he called "flat-tire Christianity," namely Christianity with the Spirit gone out of it.

With Peter's sermon filling the second half of the lesson, it might be worthwhile to look at speaking:

At a church conference the opening prayer began with: "Oh, Lord, be with the first speaker and help him to inspire those who hear your Word. And be with the second speaker and imbue her with your Spirit to share with those here. And Lord, have mercy on the last speaker."

116

On the subject of growth:

There are those who would point out that growth is unnatural for the church, Pentecost notwithstanding. It is much more natural for a church to reach a plateau and stay there. The next most natural pattern for a congregation is to decline in membership. Thus, it should be apparent that growth, either the explosive growth of the Day Of Pentecost or the slower, steady growth of the days after, is the result of both the Holy Spirit and the hard work of Christians.

Speaking of hard work and commitment to the cause of growth:

A female tourist in Florida was entranced by the necklace worn by a Seminole Indian in his native costume. She asked what it was composed of and the Indian replied it was made of alligator teeth.

"Oh, I see," the woman replied. "So it must have the same value for your people as a string of pearls has for our people."

"Not quite," replied the Indian gravely. "Anyone can open an oyster."

Approaches To Preaching

One of the themes of the Day Of Pentecost is the growth of the church. What is not always examined are the implications of that growth. First, the subject of evangelism arises. This is one of the committees in most congregations which is difficult to recruit people to serve on. Somehow the church's reluctance to evangelize has overtaken the impetus of the Spirit.

A second problem of evangelism is the assimilation of the results of evangelism, namely the new members. After the first Christian Pentecost, the church had grown by roughly 2,500 percent, which leads to questions of how to instruct the new members in the teachings of Jesus and the behaviors expected of Christians. Is it possible to be too successful? Many businesses run into significant problems when they become too successful too quickly, some even end up in bankruptcy with an extremely popular product.

Similarly, is it possible for the church to be healthy when it isn't growing? Does the community in which it finds itself matter? If it is in a growing community, or in a stable or shrinking community? What does it take to grow? The devotion and commitment of the members is a good place to start.

117

The Holy Spirit came not only to Peter, or even only to the disciples, but in fact, it included all the Christians in the room. What about the rest of the Christians? It isn't always the one out front who matters the most. In the book of Numbers, when the Spirit is shared among the seventy elders, two of them weren't with the others at the Tent of Meeting. Eldad and Medad were in the encampment when the Spirit was distributed, but they also got a share and prophesied in the camp. In many ways the same thing is happening on Pentecost. We aren't in the room for that Pentecost sharing of the Spirit, but we also get our share at Baptism, and we should prophesy and tell others about the good news.

The speaking in tongues brings up another possibility. Communication can be one of the more difficult things in a congregation. Even though it often seems as if gossip spreads just a little slower than the speed of light, other information is often difficult to spread. Newsletters are read thoroughly by only a small percentage of the recipients. Announcements in church are heard by only a percentage of the people in attendance, who are only a percentage of the membership to begin with. The gift of tongues is something that would be quite convenient in most local parishes, but the issue might be more than merely misunderstanding or inattentiveness. Are the messages really worth hearing?

Miracle Seven

Feeding The 5,000

The Text

Now when Jesus heard this, he withdrew from there in a boat to a deserted place by himself. But when the crowds heard it, they followed him on foot from the towns. When he went ashore, he saw a great crowd; and he had compassion for them and cured their sick. When it was evening, the disciples came to him and said, "This is a deserted place, and the hour is now late; send the crowds away so that they may go into the villages and buy food for themselves." Jesus said to them, "They need not go away; you give them something to eat." They replied, "We have nothing here but five loaves and two fish." And he said, "Bring them here to me." Then he ordered the crowds to sit down on the grass. Taking the five loaves and the two fish, he looked up to heaven, and blessed and broke the loaves, and gave them to the disciples, and the disciples gave them to the crowds. And all ate and were filled; and they took up what was left over of the broken pieces, twelve baskets full. And those who ate were about five thousand men, besides women and children.

The feeding miracle, specifically the feeding of the 5,000, is the only miracle which is found in all four gospels. There is some discussion over the independence of the account of the feeding of the 4,000, which is reported only in Mark and Matthew. While the details of the occurrence are questioned by many people, the basic historicity of some sort of a feeding is beyond any serious question. It is the specific details of the feeding miracle which seem to confuse the commentators and cause discussions and arguments.

Since the time of Saint Augustine the tradition has been that the feeding of the 5,000 is for the Jews while the feeding of the 4,000 is for Gentiles. Thus, the message of Jesus (and the salvation he brings) is inclusive even from the time of his public ministry. While the tradition is possibly comforting, it is somewhat contrary to the comments of Jesus in Matthew 15:24 and 26. Almost certainly the identification of a Jewish and a Gentile feeding is only a later interpretation and not something identifiable within the text itself.

About The Text

This lesson is taken out of the flow of the gospel, but the context is obscured by the selection of the lectionary. Matthew 14:1-12, the first portion of the chapter, is not included in the lectionary. This is the story of the death of John the Baptizer, which is referred to at the beginning of this lesson. While the lectionary does not provide an inclusive reading of the gospel during the Pentecost season, it does provide for a sequential arrangement of what is selected. Filling in the remaining gaps in the story is left up to the preacher.

Words
heard this — This refers to the news about John the Baptizer's death. In Matthew the death of John is the cause for the withdrawal, while in Mark 6:30-31, the withdrawal is to afford the disciples a rest after they return from their mission, recounted in Mark 5:5b-13.

deserted — The same Greek word is found in 14:15 (as well as of the wilderness in Exodus 16). The word actually means *abandoned*, or *desolate*. Traditionally translated as *lonely*, a characterization which hardly captures the sense of place found in the Greek. This term appears to refer more to the population of the area to which

120

Jesus had retreated, not the vegetation which might have been found there, especially in light of the reference to "grass" in 14:19.

by himself—The construction indicates Jesus went off alone, which raises the question of where the disciples were at this time. Clearly, this comment represents a different approach than that of Mark. Did the disciples accompany Jesus on the boat, or did they arrive later, either on their own or with the crowds? The text provides no clue to the proper answer to these questions. The text of 14:15 is of no help in this regard, as it simply indicates the disciples came up to Jesus, likely for a private discussion, not that they arrived at that point.

followed — This word is often used in the sense of "followed as a disciple," but here it likely means merely "trailed after."

on foot — Why the crowds traveled by foot is unclear. It is possible that no other boats were available, or not enough were available, or perhaps no one else was willing to transport people across the lake. Perhaps the strongest possibility is that the crowds following Jesus were composed largely of poor people, and they were unable to hire a boat for the trip.

had compassion — The term here is, literally, *entrails, viscera were stirred up.* In the ancient world, this was the idiom for affection and sympathy, or compassion, sometimes even love. Emotions were equated with body parts, a tendency that hasn't changed even in the modern world (consider the bumper stickers which begin "I heart ..."). The difference is that modern conventions do not use the same body parts as in the ancient world did.

evening — This time of day is basically indeterminate, as it can be either immediately before or after sunset. The context here suggests before, to allow time for the people to get to the villages before dark.

If the desire was to allow the people to disperse before dark, the question of what happened to them after the feeding is somewhat

121

unresolved. Matthew 14:22 begins with *immediately*, which is taken from the Marcan text. This is a favorite word of Mark's, and is more often used to indicate the commencement of a new story than the temporal sequence of events.

In Matthew 14:22-23, the crowds are dismissed, and the action moves on. The perception of an inconsistency here is based on the disciples' comments about sending the crowds away, assuming "evening" here is taken to refer to a time before dark.

came to — The Greek does not imply that the disciples arrived at this point, rather that the already-present disciples approached Jesus at this time. The likelihood is that the term indicates they drew him off to one side for a conversation.

you — The Greek behind this phrase involves both an intensifier pronoun and an imperative verb. Jesus is speaking to the disciples, and rather imperiously instructs them to feed the people themselves. At the least, this phrase should be italicized in English, perhaps in bold (even though such typographical embellishments are not often used in the biblical text).

five loaves and two fishes — These are the two elements of the basic diet for the poor in Galilee. A normal day's ration was three barley loaves (the barley is specified in John 6:9), hence this was approximately enough for two people for a day. The fish would have been either pickled or smoked, and were considered a delicacy when eaten as a relish with the bread.

sit down — The Greek is literally *lie down*, but modern diners are usually seated, hence the alteration to conform to modern practice.

grass — It sounds odd to find grass in the wilderness. We do not expect it, but Mark 6:39 has *green grass*, which would indicate spring as the time when this miracle took place. John 6:10 mentions *a great deal of grass*, which might also indicate a spring date, when the uninhabited area was growing grass that would soon be utilized for pasture. Further, John 6:4 mentions the nearness of Passover, which confirms a spring date for these events.

The place where Jesus went was most likely not a desert, but an uninhabited area considered a wilderness, land typically used for pasture when there was grass available, and largely abandoned the remainder of the year.

heaven — The Greek word can mean either *sky* or *God's residence*. Here the latter is the most likely understanding, but the former is a possibility as well. Jesus' actions here parallel both the actions of the head of a Jewish family at the beginning of a meal and of Christian leaders at the celebration of the eucharist.

blessed — This term may be taken to mean either *thanked God for the loaves and fish*, or *asked God's blessing on the loaves and fish*. Within Jewish tradition, the first meaning is precisely what the head of a family did before a meal, the second meaning is more of a modern imposition on the tradition. Hence, the first understanding is almost certainly what was intended here.

broke — The Greek word is used only for breaking bread in both the Septuagint and the New Testament. Proper etiquette required the father (head of the household) to break the bread to indicate the meal had begun. Similar to the point of etiquette in more polite times which required the person at the head of the table to place a fork on the side of the plate to indicate all at the table may begin to eat. The word was also used in breaking bread in Emmaus (Luke 24:30), and in Acts with eucharistic significance as well (Acts 2:42 and 20:7). In all four gospels there is a eucharistic significance to this miracle, indicated in large part by this word.

gave — Matthew intentionally loads the scene with eucharistic significance. Some early eucharists included both bread and fish (either in addition to the wine, or exclusive of the use of wine). In the early church the leader broke the bread, then the deacons distributed the broken pieces to the congregation.

were filled — The text here indicates a sense of *gorged*. This word is also used of the birds which gorge themselves on the flesh of slain men and animals in Revelation 19:21. The idea is of complete fullness, even from such humble beginnings as a day's food for two people. The word is also used in the beatitudes in Matthew 5:6. A modern parallel might be the feeling most people have after indulging in an all-you-can-eat buffet for lunch, or as a result of a typical, traditional Thanksgiving feast.

broken pieces — Not merely the scraps of leftover bread, but the pieces which were broken in 14:19. In other words, not only did everyone eat all they could hold, there were full portions for others remaining at the conclusion of the feeding.

five thousand men — The exact number of people is indeterminate, but at least 5,000 men were involved. Attempts to determine how many people might have been present are mostly guesswork and add little to the understanding of the event. John 6:10 reports the number of those fed as "about five thousand in all." Mark 6:44 and Luke 9:14 refer to "five thousand men," and leave the comment at that. Only in Matthew is the further detail "besides women and children" added (14:21).

Parallels

There are parallel incidents of feeding 5,000 in Mark 6:30-44; Luke 9:10-17; and John 6:1-15. In addition, there are stories of feeding 4,000 in Mark 8:1-10 and the parallel in Matthew 15:32-39. Among these six stories of the feeding of thousands, there are a number of significant parallels and omissions. In addition to the parallels already noted, some of the most significant include the following.

The most detailed account of these feedings is found in Mark. One of the earliest details found in Mark, and a fair example of what is included, is the note in Mark 6:31 indicating the disciples hadn't even had time to eat because they were dealing with the crowds coming to see Jesus.

Ironically, the lectionary selection does not include the Marcan version of the feeding miracle (or the walking on water episode which follows immediately after it). Proper 11 includes the Marcan framework for these stories, but not the stories themselves. Propers 12-16 shift to John 6, and present the longer, more theologically based Johannine versions of these stories. Only with Proper 17, and Mark 7:1 does the lectionary turn back to the Marcan version.

Luke 9:10 provides a more specific location than the other evangelists, locating the events in the city of Bethsaida, on the northern coast of the Sea of Galilee. While Luke never mentions a departure from the city, the area around the city could fit the description in Matthew. The actual feeding certainly seems to have been in a location similar to that found in the other evangelists' accounts. Luke 9:12 mentions surrounding villages, which would seem to assume a rather desolate place.

Matthew is the only gospel which isolates Jesus from disciples when the action begins. In fact, this might be a significant staging on the part of Matthew, in that the crowds seem to approach Jesus without the intermediaries normally found, namely the disciples. In this instance they approach him directly, but the feeding is accomplished through the intermediaries.

Matthew states that Jesus had compassion on the crowds and healed the sick, which is a significant editorial change from Mark's words. In Mark 6:34, Jesus has compassion, notes the crowd is like sheep without a shepherd, and teaches them. In Luke 9:11, Jesus sees the crowds and speaks to them before healing the sick. Ironically, in what has been characterized as the "Gospel of Compassion," Luke changes the Marcan wording and omits the reference to compassion at this point. Similarly, Luke and Matthew both omit the comment about sheep and shepherds. Luke does not use the comment, while Matthew has already used the comment in 9:36.

Matthew omits the Marcan reference to teaching, seemingly because in Matthew 13 Jesus has focused his teaching on the disciples. To a large extent, teaching in Matthew has, by this point, become an activity which is focused on the disciples almost exclusively, and is thus not appropriate for the large crowd at this point.

In John, when the crowd approaches, Jesus challenges the disciples to feed them with no other preliminaries. In the synoptics, a similar challenge is made but only after the preliminaries of either teaching or healing or both.

Precisely the same term (200 denarii) is used for the disciples' estimates of the cost to feed the crowd in both Mark and John. The NRSV obscures this parallel by changing the words in John, and relegating the exact wording of the Greek to a footnote. Matthew and Luke don't use precise money terms. Luke still couches the disciples' objection to the command to feed the crowds in financial (Luke 9:13) and logistical terms. Matthew simply reports the disciples' report of totally inadequate resources.

In many ways Matthew presents the most dramatic scenario. Rather than softening the disciples' actions and their reluctance to carry out Jesus' words with reasonable, quite human excuses, Matthew simply presents the disciples' human inability to comply with the demands of Jesus. Matthew presents the stark contrast between what the disciples are supposed to do, and what they are able to do, and the disciples come up woefully short, with no excuses possible.

After the disciples suggest sending the crowds away, Matthew adds Jesus' comment that they need not go away before he commands the disciples to feed them. Neither Mark nor Luke has any comment similar to this.

Mark, Matthew, and John agree that the feeding incident ended with a withdrawal by boat by the disciples. In all cases it is the disciples alone who depart in the boat, which sets the stage in these three gospels for the miraculous walking on water (which is next week's lesson). Luke has no account of the miraculous walking on water, and follows the feeding miracle with further teachings of the disciples, which Mark and Matthew also present, but only after some further activities.

As often happens, John places this event in a political context. John 6:14 indicates that the people want to make Jesus a bread messiah after the feeding. In other words, apparently because, or at least largely because of the huge amount of food which had been produced, the people declared that Jesus was the expected Messiah. The political aspects of Jesus' career, which are highlighted in the Johannine account of the feeding, are also brought up again at John 11:45-53; 12:9-11; and 18:36. Aside from the political details, John provides an immediate rationale for the departure of

Jesus from both the crowds and the disciples. In John 6:22-40 this immediate rationale is expanded into a theological discussion between Jesus and the crowds in which Jesus expands the significance of the feeding by stating "I am the bread of life" (John 6:35). This confession is both an interpretation of the recent events of the feeding and a basis for the Christian eucharistic celebrations of the time when the gospel was written.

In all three gospels, Jesus withdraws alone into the hills, in Mark and Matthew to pray.

The People

As Individuals

Jesus is obviously the most visible character, and in some ways his behavior might seem a little unexpected. There are a number of instances when Jesus, or Jesus and the disciples try to escape the crush of the crowds to have a little time for themselves. Mark makes the point that they have been so busy dealing with the people that they haven't even had a chance to grab a bite to eat (6:31). It is not a surprise that they developed a desire to escape the demands of the crowds.

When the crowds followed them, Jesus, as we might expect, was generous and welcomed them and taught them (Luke 9:11), or had compassion on them and taught them (Mark 6:34), or began to make arrangements to feed them (John 6:5), or had compassion and healed their sick (Matthew 14:14). The unexpected part of his behavior begins when he confronts the disciples over the issue of how to feed the crowd. While John (6:6) offers an excuse for this comment, in the synoptics Jesus merely commands the disciples to feed the crowd.

In many ways this demand, with no apparent means available to fulfill the requirement, is contrary to what we expect of Jesus. This is no gentle, meek Savior with hands extended to comfort his people. This is an insistent, demanding leader who suddenly demands that his followers perform things they have just declared to be impossible. If the setting is accurate, the demands come at a

127

time when everyone is probably hot, dusty (from traveling), hungry (no time to eat), cranky (from long hours), and possibly even a little jealous of the attention being lavished on the crowds when the disciples had expected to have some time alone with Jesus. Now comes an emphatic order from Jesus to feed the crowds. Over 5,000 people, and they are suddenly expected to provide an evening meal for them. The scene is not one full of the comforting images we might expect from stories about Jesus.

The disciples are almost certainly at a loss when confronted with Jesus' demands. It seems clear that there is no way to provide for the crowds from the resources at hand, and the disciples were acutely aware of the difficulties. Even if they had the resources to purchase enough food for the crowd, there was clearly no way to get the food to this remote location while there was still enough light to eat it.

When Jesus instructs them to have the crowd sit down (or recline), they finally have something to do which is within their abilities, and the situation improves when Jesus breaks the bread and tells them to distribute the pieces to the people. Aside from questions about what each disciple might have had to distribute, it is likely that the habits of a traditional Jewish mealtime took over and eliminated most questions or resentments at this time. Finally, when everyone has eaten all they want, the disciples are instructed to pick up the leftovers, and they collect twelve baskets full.

The disciples' reaction is not mentioned, nor is any reaction from the crowds (except in John, where the reaction is the attempt to declare Jesus the Messiah, which Jesus avoids). It seems likely that everyone was amazed, not only that everyone had been fed, but also at the amount of leftovers. While this had the potential to be quite a publicly-impressive miracle, it would seem that the event's timing diminished the crowd's reaction at the time, which allows the action to continue relatively unimpeded.

The crowds are favorite characters in the gospels, often used as a backdrop for the miraculous events in Jesus' public ministry. They are often, as here, the reason for certain actions, and the cause for other actions. Further, as here, the crowds are often essential participants in the action. Without them, there would, in effect, be no reason for the action. Aside from the dramatic necessities for the presence of the crowd, they are actually quite without character in this incident.

As Images And Signs

Bread, particularly barley loaves (John 6:9), were the meal of the poor. This is a clear suggestion that the followers of Jesus were generally poor. At the least, it would seem that much of the crowd following after Jesus was composed of the lowest, poorest strata of society. While this is not stated explicitly, it is likely that those who heard the story would recognize the significance of the bread which composed the bulk of the meal as a meal fit for the poorest of the folks.

An alternative understanding of bread comes from Matthew 16:5-12, where Jesus confronts the disciples who, once again, face a lack of bread, and he refers to his teaching (and that of the Sadducees and Pharisees) as bread. The bread of the Sadducees and Pharisees is contaminated by the yeast of their teaching.

Throughout the feeding story, Jesus is acting as the head of a Jewish family, both in his imperious order to provide for the crowds (an act of hospitality), and in his preparation and manner of distribution of the meal. This is an example of a ritual very familiar to those who made up the crowd, and those who initially heard the story, expanded to include an abnormally large number of individuals, but incorporating them into a familiar ritual.

As often happens, simple acts in the gospels are also signs with substantial significance. In this case, the simple act of providing food for thousands of people acts as a significant sign of larger things. To the Jews who were present, as well as those who later heard of the events, the meal was a significant messianic event. The basis for this seems to be that when the Messiah returned, there would be a parallel return to feeding the people as Moses had fed them in the wilderness (Exodus 16), a belief reflected (at a later time) in Revelation 2:17. Jesus rejects this understanding and withdraws from the crowd rather abruptly and alone (John 6:16).

The other understanding underlying the feeding is the eucharistic nature of the events. In the context of eating, a hint of the eucharist is only to be expected. Here, however, the significance is clearly intended. The blessing of the bread, the breaking and distribution not only recall the New Testament references to eucharistic meals, but also to Justin Martyr's description of the eucharist from the middle of the second century.

By the time of Justin the pickled fish had vanished from the eucharistic menu, but there is some evidence that fish was originally a part of the eucharist in some locations. This evidence includes not only the feeding miracles of the gospels, but also limited evidence in the written record, and representations scratched in the walls of the catacombs.

This eucharistic thread is present in all four gospels, even John, a Gospel which is historically misunderstood to eschew all reference to the eucharist. Even to the details of the distribution of the bread, the common practice of the early Christian church is followed in the feeding events. There is no mention of wine in any of these accounts, but it appears that not all early eucharistic celebrations used both elements.

The Action

In The Story

In the gospels the stories of miracles are typically presented with literary features which indicate the story is to be considered as an account of a miraculous happening. The stunning action of the story, and the inherently miraculous nature of the action notwithstanding, these stories are conspicuously lacking the typical literary details. The most significant omission is the failure to report any results of the miracle.

Typically the result of a miracle is the instigation of belief among at least some of the observers. Here, however, there is no astonishment at the actions, or even a hint of surprise. Even in John, where signs are accomplished precisely to bring people to faith (see, for example, John 2:11; 4:48; 7:31; 9:35-41; and 12:9-11) there is no mention of any such reaction. At the most, the reaction of the crowd is a rather self-serving one, to proclaim Jesus as

130

Messiah, seemingly to ensure a steady supply of food without the need to work for it.

Even the disciples are not reported as surprised or astonished by these events. They gather the leftovers and are hustled out of the picture. Any reaction they might have had is obscured by this quick dismissal. Some commentators have used this very absence of astonishment as a demonstration, for them, of the essentially unmiraculous nature of these events.

Thus, the question arises of whether these events should even be considered as a miracle. There are many who have argued that the true miracle is connected to the source of the food which was distributed. One school of thought argues that Jesus had caused a large supply of bread to be hidden in a convenient cave. When he withdrew, he knew the crowds would follow him, so he went to the concealed entrance to the cave and waited with the disciples. When the crowds appeared, Jesus taught and then fed them, using some of the disciples to pass the bread up from the cave to the remaining disciples for distribution. This explanation reduces the feeding miracle to a trick played by Jesus on the crowds.

An alternative is the supposition that Jesus used the supplies of the disciples and distributed them to the crowds. The selfless sharing of his only sustenance so shamed the crowds that they snuck their own supplies out of the places where they were hidden and added to the food supply as it was passed before them. Thus, as the baskets were passed, the miracle wasn't the creation of bread and fish, but the softening of hard and flinty Galilean hearts and the sharing of the resources each had brought along with their neighbor. Even if everyone wasn't actually "full" of bread and fish, each was full of a feeling of satisfaction that today, at least, they had lived up to the divine command of hospitality and care for the poor.

While both of these "explanations" have been offered as rationalistic accounts of what actually took place, there is no evidence to support such speculation. The thought that everyone would have wanted to keep a souvenir of the bread created by Jesus assumes not only a relatively modern view of these events, but also that the crowds actually knew the source of the bread, something which is equally unsupported by the text. And, it is worth pointing out that even participants often have no idea of the significance of the events they participate in. For example, during the battles in Normandy after D-Day, American soldiers called in air support against a tank in the next field which had been carefully disguised as a haystack. A pilot finally came and blew up the haystack. It was only years later that the pilot, at a reunion where he was sharing his war stories, happened to mention his strangest mission, when he was sent out to explode an inoffensive haystack. Only when one of the participants, who had been in that infantry squad on that day, and happened to be in attendance, was able to thank him for his help and explain why he had attacked that haystack — thirty odd years after the event — did he understand.

It is not difficult to suspect that many of the people in the crowd, if not most of them, perhaps all of them, had little or no idea of where the bread they were offered had actually come from. It is possible to understand the lack of the astonishment, surprise, and belief which normally follow a miracle as a demonstration that this was a miracle no one really knew as a miracle until many years later, when the stories about Jesus began to circulate more widely. A part of this lack of surprise and belief might be the result of the hurried nature of the miracle. It began about dusk, and by the time all the people had been fed, it was likely full dark, so there was almost certainly little recognition that anything miraculous had taken place at the time of the miracle. Clearly this became a favorite story, as it appears at least four times (and perhaps six times) in the gospels, with the significance of the events becoming obvious only after the events had taken place and a time for reflection had occurred.

The crowd ate and was full. Actually a very simple action, one which is gradually coming to have somewhat negative moral implications in a nation filled with obese individuals, but a sensation which was not common in the time of Jesus. An observer once commented that the most significant problem with many Civil War reenactors was that the modern people are too well fed to properly fill in for the soldiers (who were often on short rations and quite hungry) of the Civil War. The point here is, of course, the sufficiency of Jesus and his teaching for the crowd. Not only physically, but also spiritually, Jesus was able to satisfy the hungers the crowd brought to him. In many ways this is the fulfillment of Matthew's comment that "he had compassion for them and healed their sick" (14:14). He healed the whole crowd, at least at the moment, from their sickness of hunger, both their physical hunger and their spiritual hungers.

The supply of food that was distributed was overwhelming. After at least 5,000 people had been fed, there were enough leftovers to fill twelve baskets. It is likely the filled baskets indicate each of the disciples collected a basketful of leftovers, but another understanding has also been suggested. It is possible that the twelve baskets were a symbol of the refusal of Israel (and its twelve tribes) to accept the person and message of Jesus as the Messiah. Because they refused him, there were so many leftovers available for distribution to the Gentile believers who came next (see the dialog in Matthew 15:21-28).

The immense amount of food involved here would seem to underlie the eucharistic themes of the story as well. The eucharist is a table from which no one ever has to depart unfilled or unsatisfied. And, in fact, there are typically leftovers at local eucharists which derive from a traditionally strong desire to reinforce this image.

In The Hearers

The image of plenty which is a keynote of this lesson can have the effect of softening the hearts of the hearers as well as it might have softened the hearts of the participants in these events. Not only does Jesus provide healing for those who come to listen to him, he also provides bread for them. As has already been pointed out, this bread can be understood as both the physical sustenance for a day and the teaching which is specifically mentioned in Mark 6:34 and Luke 9:11. Thus, one result of hearing this story can be a softening of the hard hearts of those who hear it.

It is possible that this story also functioned as a stewardship message for the early church by reminding those who heard it of the ultimate generosity of Jesus, not merely in providing bread for those who listened to him, but in giving his life for those who

133

believed, and in giving salvation to all who follow him. There are many who seem to assume that financial matters only began to afflict the church in the modern age. Certainly, at least according to many misconceptions, there was no need to emphasize the financial aspects of following Christ in the early church.

This misunderstanding ignores substantial portions of the New Testament, including the text of Acts and various portions of Paul's writings (at the least). In fact, from the beginning of the church there was an emphasis on the way in which the generosity of Christ should serve as both an inspiration and example for the stewardship of believers. Thus, this story serves as a text for strengthening the stewardship of those who hear it.

Even before the institution of the Lord's Supper, this incident has a heavy eucharistic message. The actions are heavily influenced by the practices of the early Christians in sharing bread with each other as they were commanded on Maundy Thursday. In examining this seeming contradiction of a eucharistic emphasis before such a thing as a eucharist exists, it is helpful to remember that this gospel was written long after the eucharist began to be celebrated. The events here were structured and based on the actions of the eucharist, and certainly aroused recollections of the eucharist in those who heard the story.

The Sermon

Illustrations
There was very little food for many hungry people.

Years ago, there was a terrible earthquake in Alaska which devastated the city of Anchorage. Many people wrote to the governor of Alaska, demanding that he do certain things. Generally they outlined the suffering they had endured and wanted the state to take responsibility. After the initial surge of activity, the governor appeared on television to report to the state. Among the other letters, the governor reported he had received a 3 x 5 card from a small boy. It had two nickels taped to it and a message: "Use this wherever it is needed. If you need more, let me know."

Jesus blessed the bread.

When people travel to places where another language is spoken, one of the first (and most useful) words or phrases they can learn is the equivalent of "thank you." In Germany it is *danke schoen*; to a Spanish-speaking location, *gracias*; in French-speaking places, *merci*; where Portugese is spoken, *abrigado*; in Japan it is *spazibo*; and in Greece it is *eucharisto*. It is absolutely amazing how many ways people have to say "thank you," how useful such a phrase can be, and how rarely we remember to use the word.

Even though he was seeking a retreat from the pressures of the crowd, when the crowd appeared, he seized the opportunity to heal their sick and feed them.

Henry Ford once wrote, "A generation ago there were a thousand men to every opportunity, while today there are a thousand opportunities to every man." Is this still an accurate perception, or have things changed substantially? Do we still see opportunities everywhere, or are we trying to avoid the crowds of problems which confront us?

What were the people doing when they tried to proclaim Jesus as the Messiah in John?

In China, during the years that there was a strong missionary presence in that country, there were many "stations" where missionaries gathered converts. Converts, but not the unconverted, were baptized and then provided with food and clothing while they lived at the station. The number of converts would often rise during the times when a famine came and the only place to find food was often at the nearest mission station.

These converts, who often left as soon as the famine was over and food was readily available in other locations, came to be known as Rice Christians. Rice Christians were those who joined the church in times of need to obtain rice, but without a true acceptance of the Christian faith.

Approaches To Preaching

Clearly one of the dominant themes found in this lesson is the fullness and generosity of Christ. A huge crowd appears and as the day grows older, they are hungry. The disciples can find no way to feed them other than sending them into the villages in the area so they can buy their own food. Jesus fulfills the obligations of hospitality by having the people sit (or recline) and then providing them with food.

Imagine the difficulties in getting 5,000 people to sit and prepare for a meal. Time is slipping away, it is already dusk, and the idea is to feed everyone before it is completely dark. By the time everyone is ready to eat, the shadows must have been quite long, and the evening chill, common on spring evenings, was likely in the air. Then the disciples began distributing bread and fish to those waiting for food.

It is the stunning abundance of bread which resulted that should be so surprising to us.

There are some changes in the text to update the images — bowels are changed to compassion, lie down becomes sit down. How do we update the biblical wording to fit modern understandings, while we continue to hold the message as immutable and unchanging? One answer is that we change some of the details which help the message relate to that time so that the message relates more accurately to this time. Which means the most important question becomes how do we decide what is a detail and what is the message?

This lesson includes a very strong eucharistic message. A young man was once listening to the preacher explain the eucharist and heard him speak of the "elephants" that would be brought down the aisle. He was entranced by the prospect of such great beasts coming down the aisle, wondered where they had been kept, and wondered how they would actually participate. Some months later, in another sermon focusing on the meaning of the eucharist, the young man heard the word more accurately, and realized it was the elements that would be brought down the aisle. While his understanding had deepened and grown, he had also lost something —

the excitement of waiting for the elephants, the mystery of the details, and the joy of the image of elephants somehow taking part in the eucharist. This lesson is, in many ways, about elephants and the eucharist.

Jesus demanded the disciples should feed the crowd. In many ways this lesson turns on the disciples' inability to carry out Jesus' demand. So it is with us, as we confront the demands of the gospel and find ourselves are unable to carry out Jesus' words. The proper response to the generosity of Jesus is obviously our own generosity in giving to the church of Christ and the people of God. In the traditional formulation, the giving of our time, talents, and treasures.

Miracle Eight

Walking On Water

The Text

Immediately he made the disciples get into the boat and go on ahead to the other side, while he dismissed the crowds. And after he had dismissed the crowds, he went up the mountain by himself to pray. When evening came, he was there alone, but by this time the boat, battered by the waves, was far from land, for the wind was against them. And early in the morning he came walking toward them on the sea. But when the disciples saw him walking on the sea, they were terrified, saying, "It is a ghost!" And they cried out in fear. But immediately Jesus spoke to them and said, "Take heart, it is I; do not be afraid."

Peter answered him, "Lord, if it is you, command me to come to you on the water." He said, "Come." So Peter got out of the boat, started walking on the water, and came toward Jesus. But when he noticed the strong wind, he became frightened, and beginning to sink, he cried out, "Lord, save me!" Jesus immediately reached out his hand and caught him, saying to him, "You of little faith, why did you doubt?" When they got into the boat, the wind ceased. And those in the boat worshiped him, saying, "Truly you are the Son of God."

This miracle, in the three gospels which include an account of it, follows immediately after the feeding miracle which was the subject of the previous chapter (and the lesson for last week). In Mark, Matthew, and John these two miracles are intimately connected, and it would seem that the connection was most likely in

139

the tradition from which the gospels were formed. Thus, the full understanding of both miracles involves understanding the action of each of the miracles.

In this cycle of the lectionary, the miracles follow immediately after each other, preserving the placement found in Matthew's Gospel. In Cycle B, which generally follows Mark's Gospel, the Johannine account from John 6 is substituted for Mark's account. The Johannine account involves more detail and theological freight than the Marcan account.

Walking on water was typical of the miraculous works which were commonly reported of prophets at this time, and were, in fact, expected of a prophet. Not unlike the actions expected of a presidential candidate today, both before an announcement of the campaign and during the actual campaign (consider visits to Iowa and New Hampshire, public pronouncements on various subjects, assembling a staff, lining up campaign contributions, and so forth); prophets at the time of Jesus were expected to perform a variety of acts which were thought to certify their credentials. Walking on water was one of these actions, a feat that many presidential candidates doubtless believe they could manage if pressed to perform.

The relative privacy of Jesus' demonstration is not particularly unusual, as many of the accounts of such actions were relatively private, often leading the observers to accept the prophet and to believe in his credentials. These prophets were not necessarily Jews, as many of them were pagans, and the records of such events cover at least 100 years before the events of Christ's life.

There is a danger in studying this lesson when the student does not have a background as a sailor, or someone who is at least familiar with both the Sea of Galilee and boats. In a fierce storm such as that described, the attention of the sailors is strongly focused on the boat in which they find themselves. Things outside the boat are important only insofar as they pertain to the boat and its immediate future. The oncoming waves are critical for the way they will influence the stability of the boat, potential obstacles, such as shallow water, the shore, and materials floating on the water which might threaten the integrity of the boat. These points of focus strongly influence the understanding of this story, as it is likely that the disciples only noticed something as amazing as a person walking across the water when they had a brief respite from the storm. This supposition is strengthened by Peter's willingness to leave the boat while the storm was still raging. A number of the disciples were fishermen, and familiar with this situation from their experience. For the rest, the situation was likely completely terrifying.

About The Text

Words

Immediately — This lesson begins with a word borrowed from Mark. To understand the use here, it is necessary to understand that the original Greek text had no punctuation, no division of the text into paragraphs or chapters, not even any indication (like capital and lower case letters) of the beginning of sentences. Words were often used for this purpose, and Mark frequently uses *euthus*, *immediately* for this purpose. Thus, this first use (two further uses are discussed below) is meant simply to indicate a new incident is beginning, not an indication of the time at which it begins.

The word is omitted from a few minor witnesses, or else it was added very early by a scribe copying the text of Matthew who was familiar with Mark. In either case, the word is not a particularly big issue.

made — The Greek is very forceful here, meaning *compel someone to act* in a particular manner. In usages of this word in the rest of the New Testament, a more rounded view of the sort of compulsion involved can be seen. See, for example, Acts 26:11; 28:19; and Galatians 2:3; 2:14; 6:12. Later the word softened in meaning to include an understanding of merely *urged strongly*.

the — This is specifically the boat last mentioned in verse 13. This is one of the threads that connect the two miracle accounts.

go on ahead — The Greek here means the disciples are to go ahead of Jesus in time, not necessarily in space. This distinction allows for one naturalistic theory of what actually happens.

the other side — Matthew mentions a relatively undefined location, one that Mark had identified as Bethsaida. This identification conflicts with Luke 9:10 as to the location of the group at the time of the feeding miracle. In Luke, the group went to the region around Bethsaida to escape from the crowds. Here the disciples are headed for Bethsaida after the feeding miracle. John 6:16-17 indicates Jesus sent the disciples off to Capernaum which is located some miles along the lakeshore to the south and west of Bethsaida. These conflicting references mean that it is largely impossible to establish a precise location for either the feeding or the disciples' destination.

dismissed — This word is used of setting a prisoner free, to establish a divorce, and, here, to dismiss a crowd. It is also used as a euphemism for death.

mountain — The Greek word can mean either *mountain* or *hill*. The meaning chosen can certainly make a difference in the interpretation. It seems likely that the proper concept to use here is more on the order of a "hill" rather than a "mountain." On the other hand, the use of mountain brings back images of Moses, who fed the people of Israel in the wilderness and retreated to the mountain to commune with God. The use of the word "mountain" heightens the parallels between Jesus and Moses.

pray — This is the most common word used for praying in the New Testament. Matthew, on the other hand, reports Jesus praying only here and in Gethsemane (Matthew 26:36-46).

evening — The timing of these events is quite difficult here, unless everything happens very quickly. It was already evening (Matthew 14:15) before the people even sat down, then there was the feeding (with time to eat) and the dismissing of the disciples and the crowd.

142

Clearly evening had long since come by the time Jesus managed to get off by himself, up on a hill, to pray.

by this time — This temporal phrase indicates that when Jesus was finally alone in prayer, likely at some time after midnight, the boat carrying the disciples was in trouble. Considering the events of the day — the departure to avoid the crowds, the healings in the wilderness, the feeding, the dismissal of the disciples and the crowds, and finally a retreat for prayer — a late hour is certainly what should be expected. It is possible that from his elevation Jesus could see the boat, or he might simply have noticed the wind which had come up and, knowing the way the lake responded to such winds, was concerned.

far from land — Literally this word means *many stade*, which is a Roman measurement of approximately a furlong, which is 1/8th of a mile. On a lake, measures of distance can be tricky. Sailing many miles from a point of departure can make it seem as if a boat is far from shore, but it could be that the boat is really close to another shore of the lake or even, depending on the wind, not all that far from the point of departure. This phrase need not be taken to indicate the boat was in the geographical middle of the lake.

wind — Apparently a head wind, which made progress difficult. When sailing, boats rarely traveled directly in the direction the wind was blowing, and never directly into the wind. Most often boats sail at an angle to the wind, which makes use of the aerodynamic qualities of the sail. Depending on the characteristics of a particular boat, it is possible to sail a few degrees off the direction of the wind, when trying to travel into the wind. Thus, to travel to a destination from which the wind is blowing, it is necessary to follow a zig-zag course which eventually results in arriving at the destination. Most boats weren't able to sail very close to the wind, which meant they had to sail longer distances back and forth to accomplish a journey to a destination the wind is blowing from.

them — The wind in Matthew's account of the story is working against the boat, not the disciples. This is a poor choice of phrasing, as it seems to imply the wind is working against the disciples, not the boat.

early in the morning — Literally *in the fourth watch*, a phrase which indicates the use of the Roman method of time keeping. The Jewish system had three watches of four hours each in the night, the Romans used four watches of three hours each. Jews in Palestine at this time often used the Roman method of keeping time, so it should not be taken to mean that Matthew was overly influenced by the attributes of Roman culture as opposed to the Jewish. In any event, the heart of the incident took place sometime between 3 a.m. and 6 a.m., as dawn was approaching.

on the sea — The specific meaning of the phrase is *on the surface of the water*. The only ambiguities involved here are in some translations (not the NRSV) which have an ambiguous English construction that could be taken to mean it was the disciples who were walking on the water. The other ambiguity is in the interpretation offered by some who wish to offer a naturalistic explanation for these events and suggest Jesus was actually walking on the shore and only appeared to be walking on the water.

terrified — The verb in Matthew has changed from the Marcan word to a stronger verb. In effect, the change is from *were afraid* to *were terrified*. Fear and terror are actually not unusual reactions to manifestations of divine power in the New Testament, and particularly in the gospels, beginning, for example, with Joseph's reaction to the angel's visitation, Mary's reaction to the annunciation, and the shepherds' reaction to the angelic choir, and continuing through the reaction of Mary Magdalene and the other women in the Garden (as in Luke 24:5). This is another incident in the list of such reactions.

ghost — The Greek word *phantasma* is only used in the New Testament here and in the parallel in Mark 6:49. A common belief at

144

the time was that spirits of the night brought disaster to those who observed them, a superstition which could help sailors (who are often quite superstitious) to find the events terrifying, particularly on this night of bad winds and a storm. A fear for their lives in the midst of the storm would heighten the impact of such a completely unexpected event.

But immediately — This phrase is emphatic in Greek, here (as opposed to v. 22) indicating a temporal sequence (here as well as in v. 31). The distinction between the usage of *euthus* in verse 22 and here is that the former use initiates the recounting of the incident by connecting it to what has come before. Here, the word furthers the ongoing action without initiating a new story. As often happens, it is the context which helps the translator decipher the usage.

Take heart — This phrase is actually difficult to translate, as it seems to require a colloquial phrase which accurately reflects the Greek. "Take heart" is somewhat stilted and archaic, sounding like something which might be taken from a Tom Swift book. "Courage," as used in the TEV is not only stilted, but brings in bad connotations of possible works of righteousness on the part of the disciples. If the phrase wasn't somewhat archaic, a good choice might be "Buck up, boys." Perhaps something on the order of "Hang tough, guys," is a more modern phrasing.

It is I — This is an *ego emi* phrase in the Gospel of Matthew, paralleling the use in Mark 6:50. Jesus is using the name of God to identify himself. While this phrase is often identified in John as significant (and it is used in John 6:20), it is usually overlooked when used in the synoptics. As all three accounts record this phrase, it seems reasonable to conclude that this is meant to be a verification of the divinity of Christ, as demonstrated by his walking on the water.

do not be afraid — This phrase is a better translation than *don't be afraid*. The contraction is weaker in English than the expanded form, and here the phrase is a corrective for the disciples' terror.

Lord — Perhaps it is surprising that this word is actually ambiguous in this place. Is it a confession of the lordship of Christ, which seems out of place before the storm has actually been quieted, or is it merely the honorific use (i.e. *sir*) which is an alternate understanding of the Greek (and often the more appropriate if less reverent translation)? Most likely the latter, but translations usually opt for the more reverent word choice, even if it causes a blurring of the actual theology of the text.

the water — This word is actually *the waters* in Greek, apparently a Hebraism, as the plural is used exclusively in the Old Testament (and most often translated into a singular form in English) to refer to bodies of water.

noticed — The Greek verb is *blepon*, or *he saw*. Apparently this is an example of figurative language in Greek as it is usually quite difficult to "see" the wind. On the other hand, as a fisherman who spent most nights on the water, Peter would be quite familiar with the various signs which betray the strength of the wind such as the behavior of the waves, the breeze on his cheek, the stretch of the sails, and so on. It would be entirely natural and virtually unnoticed for him to be aware of these things, what is unusual is that seemingly he doesn't notice anything until he is actually walking on the water toward Jesus.

sink — The verb here is used only by Matthew in the New Testament, here and in Matthew 18:6. The second use is Jesus' comment in response to the disciples' question about greatness in the kingdom. After calling the disciples to humility like a child's, he informs them that anyone who puts a stumbling block in front of someone who is a "little one," would be better off with a millstone around his neck and downing (or sinking) in the sea. In both these uses, the sinking involves connotations of drowning.

save — The same word is used, in similar circumstances, in Matthew 8:25. In that place the disciples and Jesus are in a boat, on the sea, and a storm comes up. The disciples are again terrified, and they call of Jesus to "save us!" Here the expression of the need has narrowed to only Peter.

You of little faith — This is one word in Greek, an adjective used substantively. It could be rendered "faithless one," or in an even more disparaging fashion. Certainly it is a term of disfavor applied to Peter.

why did you doubt? — Translated literally, this phrase could be rendered *why into doubt?* Faith, in Greek, requires *eis* (*into*) to indicate the object of faith, a linguistic assumption that faith is inevitably lodged in something. In a manner evocative of that assumption, and in contrast to faith, Jesus asks, "Why into doubt?" which could be understood as "Why did your faith turn into doubt?"

doubt — The word is used only here and in Matthew 28:17 in the New Testament. Doubt is the primary meaning of the word, although *waver* and *hesitate* are also offered as possible translations. In many ways the alternatives can be understood as amplifications of the Greek understanding of what doubt was composed of.

ceased — The wind died down, or abated. It should be noted that a dead calm, the result of the wind ceasing completely, could be just as problematic to the disciples' progress across the lake as a howling gale. It is more likely the image here is of a wind which settles down to a gentle breeze, a friendly wind which drives the boat toward its destination.

worshiped — This word means more than just *honored*, which is one optional meaning of the word. Disciples responded to Jesus' implicit claim of divinity in both his actions (walking on water) and his words (*ego emi*, using the name of God to announce his identity) and treated Jesus as God, i.e. worshiped him.

Parallels

While this incident of Jesus walking on the water is found in Mark, Matthew, and John, Peter's challenge to Jesus and his subsequent action in walking on the water are found only in Matthew. The broad outlines of all three accounts are similar.

Shortly after a feeding, the disciples leave Jesus and go off in a boat. In Mark and Matthew, Jesus sends them away before going into the hills; in John, they leave after Jesus withdraws to the hills.

While Jesus is in the hills praying, the winds come up and the boat is in trouble in the rough seas. The disciples are quite terrified, but then Jesus comes to them walking on the water. He announces his identity with the name of God (*ego emi* in Greek) and tells the disciples not to be afraid.

In Matthew, Peter then seems to be filled with bravado and issues a challenge to Jesus. If the person walking toward the boat is, in fact, Jesus, then he should be able to permit Peter to walk on the water as well. At the least, this is what Peter's comment sounds like. While it is difficult to "hear" the tone of voice in a written comment, but the effort in this case is worth it. If Peter is indeed issuing a challenge, it is quite easy to hear large amounts of disbelief in the identity of the person walking across the water. Perhaps, as the disciples first assumed (in Mark and Matthew), he still believes the figure is a ghost, and is demanding further proof of his identity. In this case, we should hear the comment in a taunting, challenging tone, perhaps in a voice of insolent bravado.

An alternative is suggested by Peter's response to the simple invitation, "Come." Apparently with no hesitation, Peter got out of the boat and began walking on the water toward Jesus. If the challenge was delivered as a demand for further identification, some hesitation and backfilling at the side of the boat might reasonably be expected. In fact, Jesus would have answered the challenge by calling Peter and forcing him to walk on the water with him. If the figure was a ghost, and it had given the same answer, Peter could step off the boat and sink immediately below the waves. Without both recognition and faith in the figure out on the water, Peter's actions would have been not merely foolhardy, but close to suicidal. However, he seems to have acted quickly and decisively,

148

which suggests strongly that his challenge was actually a humble request to be allowed to share in the experience of walking on the water, even if only through the agency of Christ. In this instance we must hear the question as a simple request, spoken in as humble a voice as the weather conditions allowed.

The validity of this latter understanding of Peter's comment is supported by his subsequent actions. Peter scrambles out of the boat and walks toward Jesus. Then, when the realization of his position and what he was doing began to sink in, Peter began to sink below the waves. Jesus then addresses him as "You of little faith," which seems to be an explanation of why Peter was unable to continue his walk to Jesus. Jesus must save him and bring him back to the surface.

Finally, in Matthew, Jesus and Peter get into the boat. In Mark, Jesus alone gets in, while in John, the disciples want Jesus to get in (but the actual boarding of the boat is unreported). In John, the boat was immediately transported to the immediate vicinity of their destination. In Mark and Matthew, the winds die down after Jesus enters the boat. In Mark, the disciples were astounded, but still without understanding of either the significance of the feeding or the walking on the water. In Matthew, the disciples worship Jesus (accepting his self-description) when the wind ceased.

There is a further incident which might be taken as a parallel. In Mark 4:35-41, there is an account of another trip on the lake, this time with Jesus and the disciples together. In the course of the crossing Jesus falls asleep before a wind kicks up and the boat is threatened with swamping. The disciples wake Jesus (addressing him as "Lord") and he rebukes them for their lack of faith (in Matthew, before he stills the storm; in Mark and Luke, after the winds cease). Then he calms the sea and the disciples are quite respectful, awed, and filled with a godly fear at this revelation of the authority of Jesus.

In its outline at least, this earlier stilling of the storm by Jesus does seem to be similar to the present episode. The differences between the two accounts (Jesus' presence on the boat, no connection to a feeding story, and the questions about the faith of all the disciples) are probably indications of the disparate sources of the accounts. The surface similarities can be attributed to a tendency to make the stories more similar as they were transmitted.

The differences between the accounts in Mark and Matthew are also quite significant. In Mark, it is the disciples who personally are in danger, in Matthew it is the boat (a symbol of the church) which is endangered. In Mark, Jesus apparently meant to pass the disciples by, seemingly to hurry across (or around) the lake and meet them at their destination. If this is the case, then the miracle is an unplanned, spontaneous, and accidental event. That it is even included is a further accident.

In Matthew 14:24 it is "the boat, battered by the wave ... far from the land" which draws Jesus' attention. Historically a boat has long been used as a symbol of the church. Even in pagan times a boat or ship was a symbol of joy and happiness, also as a depiction of the means by which salvation was to be accomplished, a meaning which leads quite naturally to the use of a ship or boat as a symbol of the church. In Matthew this understanding of the boat seems quite appropriate here, particularly as a symbolic presentation of the way in which the risen Christ is available to assist the church in its time of trouble.

The exact itinerary of the boat is quite unclear. In Mark, the destination is Bethsaida, but Luke places the feeding miracle in the area of Bethsaida. In John, the destination of the boat trip is Capernaum, which is some miles down the lakeshore from Bethsaida. Matthew opts for a nonspecific destination, and reports the disciples get into the boat and head for the "other side." Mark 6:53 and Matthew 14:34 have disciples disembarking in Gennesaret, which is south of Capernaum on the lakeshore. The healings at Gennesaret, which is the next story in Mark and Matthew, is an incident John does not mention.

In addition to opting for a generic destination, Matthew also removes Mark's comment about the disciples' failure to understand about the loaves which concludes the Marcan narrative (Mark 6:51-52). Mark reports that the disciples' hearts were still hardened, while in Matthew the disciples finish the episode worshiping Jesus. While this is understandable as a response to the use of the name of God by Jesus to identify himself (Matthew 14:27), it is also a sign of the disciples' awareness of the special status of Jesus. Contrary to Mark's perception, in this gospel the disciples clearly understand Jesus' role.

The People

As Individuals

Normally in the gospels it is Jesus, or perhaps Peter, who is presented in the greatest relief. The disciples are almost like cardboard figures who fill in the background without really adding much to the story, and certainly not adding much individual definition. In this story Jesus is the least detailed figure, Peter is still foremost, but the disciples, at least in Matthew's account, are quite easily recognizable as human figures, and actually very sympathetic.

It had been a long, weary stretch. The disciples had gone out preaching the message of the kingdom, and returned to Jesus about the time John the Baptizer had been killed. Not merely tired, but also quite likely a little concerned about this turn of events (not to mention grief stricken by the murder of John), they had sought to go off alone for a brief time to regroup (Matthew 14:13). The crowds would have none of it, they followed the group closely, and when they arrived at the place the group had found, Jesus healed their sick and then demanded that the disciples furnish the crowd with food. Eventually, as darkness descended on the whole scene, the crowds were fed miraculously. Then Jesus hurried the disciples into the boat they had used to cross the sea and, as the blackness of the night settled in, sent them out on the sea. Finally, he sent the crowds away and went away on his own, into the hills to be alone.

After the long trying days they had just passed through, it is not a surprise that the disciples, many of whom were familiar with both boats and the Sea of Galilee from their background as fishermen, could have missed any signs of impending bad weather. At the most, they might have been filled with a vague unease over the hurried departure and leaving Jesus alone with the crowds. But they made steady progress across the water. Perhaps they were drowsy, almost certainly the non-sailors were, by this time.

151

Then the storm came up. Storms can arise on the Sea of Galilee quite quickly, and the disciples familiar with the ways of the lake would rightly have been very concerned. The sudden storms could be vicious; swamping boats, and drowning their crews. Certainly all of the fishermen in the boat, and probably at least some of the others had known people (or had known of people) who had died in such storms. Now it looked as if their time had come. All the concern of the past days overwhelmed them in the howling wind, and they struggled hopelessly with the sails to control the boat.

Then a ghostly figure approached them, walking on the top of the water. Even though this lesson is appointed for early in August, it has at least this element which evokes Halloween. A spooky figure, likely glimpsed by a non-sailor first (the sailors' focus had certainly narrowed to the boat itself in their effort to survive the wind and waves), was heading toward them. Perhaps seen first in glimpses as the boat rose to the crest of a wave, then the figure vanished as the boat slid down into the trough between the waves. A figure in light colored robes was so unexpected that the first disciples to see it were certainly terrified by the approach of what they assumed to be a ghost, a spirit that would kill them even if they didn't drown when the ship was broken up by the wind and waves.

The terror of the first disciples to see the figure spread quickly to the rest of the group, so that they were all terrified by the time the figure approached within hailing distance. Finally close enough that a conversation might reasonably be carried on, even in the howling wind, and still with no real signs that the figure was someone they might know, the terror increased. The disciples were afraid of drowning, and here came a figure who was obviously master of the waves, perhaps coming for their lives. After all, people rarely saw ghosts and lived to tell the story, so it was easy to assume that simply seeing a ghost meant you were marked for death.

And then, in a crescendo, the ghost speaks, and they all recognize the voice. Even before the meaning of the words sinks in, the voice is familiar to all the disciples. Amazingly enough, it isn't a ghost walking across the water. It's Jesus! Imagine the relief the

152

disciples must have felt at that realization, that they weren't going to die. The ghost wasn't an enemy, but the Lord. Even as he spoke, his voice had begun to dispel the disciples' terror, even before they grasped the words.

Peter was clearly the most forward of the disciples, and perhaps slightly more quick-witted than the others. Perhaps, he had assumed the role of captain when the boat was threatened, and the other disciples were still deferring to that authority as the identity of the ghost became apparent. In any event, Peter called out to the ghostly figure of Jesus and asked to join him. Jesus told Peter to come, and Peter quickly climbs out of the boat onto the still-raging waters. But after a few steps he realized the utter, absolute incongruity of his position on top of the waves and began to sink. He certainly felt the rush of returning terror as he cried out, "Lord, save me!"

And Jesus saved him, but also rebuked him for his loss of faith. Chastened, Peter climbed into the boat with Jesus, the storm quieted, and the voyage to Gennesaret continued. The disciples in this story are rather completely human, their actions are totally understandable, and the conclusion of the story with their worshiping of Jesus is absolutely acceptable as both a recognition of the authority he embodied and their relief at the sudden removal of the threat to their lives.

Peter acts in a way we might expect from the other stories about him in the gospels. He is a leader, speaking for the disciples in recognizing Jesus. He is quick to say things which sound very brave, as in his request to walk on the water with Jesus. He ends up having problems and needing help to be saved, when he actually climbs out of the boat, walks, and sinks.

Jesus, in this episode, is the least well-defined character. For unexplained reasons he sends the disciples away. The Gospel of John offers the threat of a political claim which might have been very enticing to the disciples. It is certainly possible that Jesus dismissed them to get them away from that temptation, but such a rationale is not stated in this gospel. Jesus then goes off alone to pray.

After a time he came walking across the water toward the boat which had become embroiled in a storm. There is no further explanation for this, simply a bald statement that he was walking on the water. Matthew clearly was not bothered by any desire to provide a naturalistic explanation for how such a thing could occur, and even though it is sometimes difficult, perhaps this is the best way to approach this episode — not getting bogged down in the details of how the events could have happened. After an exchange with Peter, Jesus (and Peter) climbed into the boat and Jesus accepted the worship of the disciples. Not only is his behavior in this story unusual in the gospel accounts, in that he accepts the worship of the disciples, but there is not a clue about why Jesus acts in the way he does. There is no compassion here, no desire to instruct, not even any indication that he came across the lake to rescue the disciples. In many ways the figure of Jesus in this episode is quite mysterious and difficult to approach.

As Images And Signs

The most obvious image of this lesson in that of the boat, which is symbolic of church. Jesus comes across the sea to save the church and the church responds by worshiping Christ. While this requires seeing the story as an allegory, the interpretation is not particularly far-fetched or strained, and does offer a number of insights for the attentive listener or reader.

Shortly after the feeding (which can be taken as a reference to the eucharist), the disciples are sent off in a boat while Jesus goes off by himself. Similarly, shortly after the institution of the eucharist on Maundy Thursday, the church is sent off on its own while Jesus goes off by himself (crucifixion, ascension, Pentecost). Thus, the church is traveling through the world seemingly without Christ, at least without a visible Christ. In this situation, the church is often fearful, even terrified with depressing regularity.

Into this picture, where the church seems to be threatened with utter destruction, a fearful image comes across the waves to bring the church salvation. Even though there are still problems in the church (even among those who lead the church, as Peter led the disciples), Jesus is truly with the church to still the storms which terrify it, bringing peace and tranquility, and accepting the worship offered by those within the boat of the church.

This understanding is rooted in a view of this story, in fact in this section of the gospel, as being more connected to the life of the church after the ascension. While this seems difficult to accept, the simple fact is that Matthew has no way to comment on the life of the church except by placing stories in his narrative that can be understood as explaining how the church works after Christ has physically left the scene.

The word "immediately" is used three times in this lesson. The first time it is used as it is often used, to introduce new events into the narrative. This is a sort of verbal punctuation to indicate the beginning of a new incident and might not even need to be translated, as, in fact, it is not in the New American Bible.

The second occurrence of the word is in response to the terror of the disciples, when Jesus acts quickly to reassure them. Clearly the effort succeeded, since the disciples recede into the background and Peter asks to walk to Jesus.

The third occurrence is during Peter's stroll on the water, when his terror returns and he begins to sink. Jesus immediately reaches out and catches Peter, saving him from sinking below the waves. These three uses can be taken to highlight the concern for the church which Jesus has displayed in the past, and which can be expected in the future.

The Action

In The Story

The reason Jesus sends the disciples out in the boat is somewhat problematic. Is this simply to set up events the next morning? While this is certainly a possible understanding, the Marcan version strongly implies the encounter on the water was accidental, not planned. Matthew has done little to indicate the encounter is intended. In both gospels it seems the plan was for Jesus to arrive at the destination before the disciples arrived in the boat. It happened that Jesus was noticed by the disciples accidentally.

155

Is this action meant as a decoy for the crowds, to lead them to believe that everyone had departed in the boat? While this sounds very like a way to gain a brief respite from the demands of the crowds, the idea founders on the second half of Matthew 14:22, where it is reported that Jesus dismissed the crowds personally.

Perhaps the best suggestion is based on the situation detailed in John and the desire of Jesus to get the disciples out of the way. John explains that the crowds desired to proclaim Jesus as the bread messiah. This development, in John, occurs before the disciples leave, but without any indication the disciples were aware of it. John does report Jesus' withdrawal into the hills before the disciples' departure in the boat, however (John 6:14-17).

In Matthew, it seems that Jesus might be hustling the disciples away from the crowds before the disciples joined with the crowds in proclaiming him a bread messiah. It explains the need to get the disciples off the shore and Jesus' subsequent dismissal of the crowds. By that time, as John 6:17 states explicitly, it was dark. It is possible that the darkness explains the sequence of events in Matthew as well, as it would be much easier for a single person to slip away in the darkness than for Jesus and the twelve to all slip away from the crowds without being noticed.

Sailing after dark would not necessarily be a difficult thing for the disciples, since they were fishermen, and as fishermen normally went out at night to ply their trade.

The action of this story evokes the Old Testament in at least two ways. First, in the more general way that recognized God as the master of seas, storms, and thunder. More specifically, there are at least three episodes in the Old Testament which involve a miraculous path through water — crossing the Red Sea (Exodus 14:21-32), the passing of Israel over the Jordan (Joshua 3-4), and Elisha's crossing of the Jordan (2 Kings 2:11-14). Even though these episodes do not involve walking on the water, but rather parting the water to provide dry ground to walk upon. These events have been associated with this episode of Jesus' life from ancient times.

In more recent times there has been an effort to discover a naturalistic explanation of the events described here, an explanation which does not require the abandonment of any natural laws.

These explanations include both walking on the shore and the idea that the whole incident is an allegory which never really took place. If that is to be understood, then in the intense darkness just before the dawn comes, Jesus was walking along the shore of the sea, and the boat was driven in close to the shore, almost to the point of destruction. In this version of events Peter jumped off the boat, and either sank immediately; or, swimming and wading, made his way to Jesus; or, was overwhelmed by a wave, which Jesus pulled him through. Clearly, Peter's doubts would be quite likely to resurface shortly after he left the boat in any of these scenarios.

Ultimately, these naturalistic explanations are not completely satisfying. Even though it is difficult to conceive of the physics required to enable Jesus to actually walk on the surface of the water (not to mention Peter, at least for a few steps), it is likely that the actions as described in Matthew need to be simply accepted as a report of what took place. The theological content of the story should not distract from the events which are reported in three gospels.

The action of these two stories, the feeding and the walking on water, when taken together seems to present quite a prophetic theology. Here we have the sacred meal to strengthen the believers, and a sign of the comforting presence of Jesus when things are difficult and terrifying. These events can easily be taken as a foreshadowing of the events of Maundy Thursday and Pentecost and beyond. This theological understanding is certainly hinted at in the Marcan account, and more highly developed in both Matthew and John, not to mention the extension of the idea in next week's lesson.

In The Hearers

The use of the term "Lord" to address Jesus is so normal that it is most often ignored, yet in this story it is used with a different implication each time Peter uses the word within three verses. The first use, in Matthew 14:28, shows Peter filled with bravado after Jesus identifies himself and the disciples realize he isn't a ghost. In this instance the term is used with a meaning much closer to "Sir" than the reverence which is usually heard in "Lord." It is almost as if Peter is still harboring some doubts about the identity of this apparition which has appeared, and suspects it might be trying to trick him in some way.

When Jesus responds to Peter's challenge by inviting him to join him on the water, Peter jumps over the side of the boat and walks toward Jesus. Then, when his situation sinks in, Peter begins to sink into the sea and shouts out "Lord" for a second time. This use is substantially more reverent, certainly quite close to a prayer, at the least a sudden plea for help. The second use is more rightly translated as "Lord" than the first, a distinction which hearers in a society with significant class distinctions, often based on heredity would understand more naturally.

The second use also functions in a literary manner to usher in the point that Jesus is Lord, even over the elements of a storm (a point made explicitly in Matthew 8:27). Here the nature of Jesus' lordship is not stated explicitly, but is rather the lead-in to the act of worship which follows.

This worship of Jesus is the structural climax of the episode, and it is often approached as more of an afterthought than an important part of the narrative. This is an example of the validation of the miracle, namely in the reaction of the disciples in being brought to the worship of Christ. By bringing out this point, the story took on a deeper meaning for the people who first heard the story. More than a story in the tradition of prophetic leaders who walked on the water, more than a further example of Jesus' authority over nature, this is an episode which includes two miracles (walking on water and stilling the storm) which lead the disciples to a stronger faith in Jesus and to the expression of that faith in their worship.

The Sermon

Illustrations

Martin Luther once said:

"Birds lack faith. They fly away whenever I enter the orchard, though I mean them no ill. Even so do we lack faith in God."

158

Faith in the face of stress can be a difficult thing.

There was a young soldier in Italy who leapt into a foxhole just an instant before a hail of bullets passed over him. He nervously began digging the hole deeper and heard the sound of metal rubbing on metal. Digging through the dirt, he found a silver crucifix which had likely been left there by a former occupant of the foxhole. Just then, another soldier came tumbling into the hole. As the two residents sorted themselves out, the young soldier noticed the new arrival was a chaplain. Holding out the crucifix, he said, "Quick, show me how to use this thing."

Churches are still involved in situations we might call disasters.

There was once a small midwestern newspaper which printed the announcement — "We are pleased to announce that the cyclone which blew away the Methodist church last Friday did no real damage to the town."

Peter began to walk on the water quite enthusiastically. Here's a view of enthusiasm.

A football coach from the days of Knute Rockne was once giving a pep talk to his players during halftime of a game they were losing by a large score. Building up to the climax of the speech, the coach pointed to the door at one end of the locker room and shouted to his team: "And now, let's go through that door and on to victory!"

In response to the inspiring speech, the team stood as one person and rushed through the door the coach had pointed at. They rushed through, and ran right into the swimming pool.

There is a relationship between faith and prayer. Jesus withdrew to pray, Peter had problems with his faith. The same thing can happen today.

There was once a town afflicted with a serious drought, and the local churches got together for a prayer meeting to beseech God for an end to the drought. Someone noticed that a young girl was the only person who brought an umbrella.

Approaches To Preaching

Why into doubt? The literal rendering of Jesus' question is actually quite a stunning theological question, one which accuses us all. In addition to the parallels between this question and the Greek word for faith, it is important to note the Jesus did not say Peter's faith wasn't enough. He simply asked "Why into doubt?" Apparently Peter's faith had deserted him and he had descended into doubt. This is not a matter of being a few bricks short of a house, but a matter of having no shelter.

The reaction of the disciples to the sudden appearance of Jesus was terror. This is a common reaction in the Bible, particularly in the New Testament. It is also a common reaction to sudden evidence of God's presence even today. The sudden revelation of divine power upsets our lives, and the events which cause terror can cause it for a variety of reasons. The most important aspect of this approach is to avoid being judgmental in the sermon to be delivered.

It is tempting to dwell on the image of Jesus withdrawing from the crowds to pray. This is a temptation which should likely be avoided, at least in this cycle of lessons. Jesus is only reported as praying twice in the Gospel of Matthew, which is hardly the best basis for a sermon encouraging a strong devotional life.

A howling wind is a terrifying experience. Anyone who has ever faced a wind this fierce is a willing witness to the fear it can inspire. However, some wind is needed to propel the boat toward its destination. It is the issue of the amount of wind at a given time which is important, that can lead to an expectation that some wind is essential and we can expect that there will be some wind, some storms in our lives. It will likely be terrifying at times, but Jesus is still with us.

Peter is called the "faithless one." After his confession at Caesarea Philippi, he is called "Satan" (Matthew 16:23). Of course, he eventually denies even knowing Jesus. Even with his lapses and difficulties with this faith he had embraced, Peter is still the leader

160

of the disciples. We seem to think any failing is enough to disqualify a leader, but it probably shouldn't be that way. Certainly a single failing shouldn't be taken as something that will disqualify us from ever being accepted by God.

The boat is the church, and after the crucifixion Jesus seems to be separated from the church. In the ensuing time, the church faces storms of persecution and other problems. It can be easy to forget Jesus is, in fact, still with the church. The incident of Peter walking on the water and sinking into it is a quite appropriate topic for preachers, and likely was used quite early as an object lesson about the dangers of faithlessness. The account here might have been influenced by the preaching of the early church.

Proper 15   Matthew 15:21-28
Pentecost 13
Ordinary Time 20

Miracle Nine

The Demon-Possessed Girl

The Text

*Jesus left that place and went away to the district of
Tyre and Sidon. Just then a Canaanite woman from that
region came out and started shouting, "Have mercy on
me, Lord, Son of David; my daughter is tormented by a
demon." But he did not answer her at all. And his disciples came and urged him, saying, "Send her away,
for she keeps shouting after us." He answered, "I was
sent only to the lost sheep of the house of Israel." But
she came and knelt before him, saying, "Lord, help me."
He answered, "It is not fair to take the children's food
and throw it to the dogs." She said, "Yes, Lord, yet even
the dogs eat the crumbs that fall from their masters'
table." Then Jesus answered her, "Woman, great is your
faith! Let it be done for you as you wish." And her
daughter was healed.*

There is a danger in the lectionary. Focusing on a series of
lessons can make it difficult to look beyond the lesson at hand to
see what comes before and what follows for the further explication
of today's lesson. The lesson at hand, the healing of a woman's
daughter, is a good example of this problem. On this day there is
an optional portion of the lesson. Matthew 15:10-20 may be read
before the lesson appointed for the day (the story actually begins at
Matthew 15:1, but it is slightly truncated in the lectionary). The
optional portion is a discussion of what makes a person clean or
unclean.

163

While such a discussion is not common today, and certainly not in the sense of ritual purity which underlies the original discussion, it does put the healing in today's appointed lesson in a sharper focus. The woman seeking the miracle is clearly unclean, actually beyond the concept of ritual purity as she is introduced as a Canaanite and hence is totally unworthy of receiving a miracle. Yet, she ends up with a daughter who is healed at Jesus' command.

This is also the third week in a row when faith is an issue in the Gospel Lesson. The first week, it was a matter of faith to follow Jesus' directions and have the people sit down so all 5,000 of them could be fed with five loaves and three fish. Last week it was the faith of Peter when he walked on and then sank into the water. Now it is the immense faith of a pagan woman.

This is also the fourth miracle in a group of miracles (beginning with the feeding of the 5,000, followed by the walking on water, healings at Gennesaret, this miracle, the healing of some sick people, and concluding with the feeding of the 4,000) which can be understood as a presentation of Jesus as the Lord of the church, singling out Peter as the leader (and successor of Jesus), and establishing the disciples as the ministerial agents charged with carrying on the continuing ministry of Christ. This series of miracles can be understood as Matthew's explanation of the pattern of growth on the church after the resurrection and ascension.

About The Text

Words

that place — The last place mentioned is Gennesaret, from Matthew 14:34, and it seems to be the place referred to here.

the district of Tyre and Sidon — Tyre is about thirty miles to the northwest of Gennesaret, Sidon about 25 miles north of that. The preposition used here (the Greek word *eis*) can be taken to mean *to* or *toward* when used with terms indicating a place. Thus the text does not actually support the understanding that Jesus went to either city. At the most, it is the district, not necessarily the cities themselves which is the location for these events.

The further question comes up, in light of the remainder of the episode, of what Jesus was doing in pagan territory (namely the district of Tyre and Sidon). This is the only incident in this gospel where Jesus might be understood to have gone into pagan territory, but the text could also be understood to mean he merely went toward the district and did not actually enter it.

Matthew also mentions Tyre and Sidon in 11:21-24, and it has been suggested as a result that he might be writing his gospel (at least in part) to a church in that area.

Canaanite — By this time there is no longer any geographical area known as Canaan. Is the term being used as a generic designation for residents of Phoenicia (Tyre and Sidon)? Josephus writes of the strong (negative) feelings of the residents of Tyre toward Jews only a few years after the time of Jesus, which adds an extra undercurrent to the present story. It is a dramatic heightening of events to find a woman of such faith in such an unlikely place, when the events of the Passion are looming on the horizon (when the Jews, who should be faithful, will generally be found to be faithless). The word is a *hapex legomenon* in the New Testament, although the term is frequently used in the Old Testament (when there was actually a geographical and ethnological referent for the use).

came out — The same verb was used earlier for *left* (Matthew 15:21), which calls into question the details of the location of this miracle. Did Jesus enter the Gentile territory or did the woman "come out" of that territory to meet Jesus within the Jewish territory of Galilee? The text is unclear, although the Jerusalem Bible, in a note, presents this understanding as the appropriate way to understand this text.

Lord — This use could be either the honorific, *sir*, or the reverent title regularly applied to Jesus, *Lord*. While the second use is quite common in this gospel, it is possible to hear the woman, not being a Jew, using the title without knowing the meaning it has in a

Jewish setting. Perhaps she heard others using the title in addressing Jesus, or perhaps she had been told by others she should call him by this title. There is at least a mild note of irony here that a Canaanite (even a Canaanite woman) would actually use such a title to address a Jewish holy man, with the implication of subservience inherent in the title.

Son of David — If the title "Lord" is ironic, this title is rather strange in the mouth of a Canaanite woman. It is a Jewish messianic title with significant political overtones. It is fairly uncommon for anyone in the gospel to use such a title. Prior to this use, the term appears in the genealogy, as an angelic address to Joseph, and twice in reference to Jesus. After this, the term is used five separate times, most notably by the crowd during the entry into Jerusalem. It is the political nature of the term in that context that helps to explicate the eventual sentence of death for the political crime of attempted usurpation of the throne. It is certainly unusual for a Canaanite woman to use such a term.

tormented by a demon — This term literally means "terribly possessed." It is a very pithy phrase in Greek, only a verb and adverb. It is not particularly easy to translate, and a variety of translations are possible. It can be rewarding to examine different translations to compare the wording selected for more insight.

came — The disciples gathered closer around Jesus, not that they had just arrived from somewhere else.

urged — This translates an imperfect tense, which includes an understanding of the continuing nature of the asking, hence the possibility of translating the word as either *begging* or *nagging*. Clearly the disciples are mightily bothered by the woman.

Send her away — An alternate translation could be "Give her what she wants." As the simplest way to get rid of her, the alternate presents a natural and logical way to understand the disciples' comments. If this translation is selected, the disciples are very much like a person confronted with a ragged person on the street who asks for spare change. A quick hand into a pocket and the distribution of some change is the very embodiment of this sentiment (and the antithesis of true stewardship and giving).

The harsher translation is a better fit with what comes after the disciples' comment. This is clearly not a sign of any compassion or sympathy for the woman's situation on the part of the disciples, but an expression of their exasperation with a woman who has managed to become a pain in various parts of their anatomy.

the lost sheep of the house of Israel — There are two potential translations of this phrase. First, as it appears, which utilizes *the house of Israel* as a modifier of the *lost sheep*. In other words, in answer to the question which sheep, the phrase responds the ones from the nation of Israel.

Alternatively, the phrase could be rendered *the lost sheep, the house of Israel* which equates the two phrases and makes the second a restatement and amplification of the first, not a modification.

came — This word highlights the difficulties of producing an exact sequence of these events. First, what are Jesus and the disciples doing when the lesson starts — sitting, standing, or walking? The text provides no clear answer.

The comment by the disciples, "after us," certainly seems to indicate the group is in motion, but Jesus' comment to her could take place either as they continued to walk (a rather curt dismissal), or it could indicate the group had stopped. This verb is a bit out of place, as it seems to say the woman was still chasing after the group. But if this was the case, exactly what were the mechanics of events when she knelt?

knelt — This word, in Greek, means considerably more than merely bending a knee in front of someone. Literally the word means *prostrate*, or *bow down to kiss* (as in kissing someone's feet). Clearly the word has more of a connection to worshiping Jesus than the simple act of kneeling seems imply. In Matthew 14:33

the disciples were worshiping Jesus, now a Gentile and a woman seems to be doing the same.

Lord — Once again, the issue is the proper translation of the term. Even though *sir* is a very probable translation, the reverent term *Lord* is also very possible, especially in light of the woman's posture when she spoke.

fair — In Greek, *kalos*, which has a root meaning of *good*, or *beautiful*, and a generally accepted meaning of *healthy*, *sound*, or *fit*. Some manuscripts have a reading with a word meaning *lawful*, but scholars generally agree this is a later attempt to strengthen the rationale for Jesus' rather callous sounding reply.

food — Literally this word means *bread* — which was the basic component of the diet at this time and often used as a synonym for the more generic term *food*.

throw — The word does not indicate an effort to drive the dogs away, but to feed them with the table scraps taken directly from the table.

dogs — Apparently this term means something on the order of *house dogs*. Not exactly *pets* in the way the term is understood today, as house dogs would generally have to earn their keep in some way. The word translated here is generally understood as a diminutive of the word used to indicate the dogs of the street or fields, i.e., wild dogs.

At the time dogs were regarded as unclean animals, the ones which, along with pigs, ate human filth. Figuratively, "dogs" was often used to refer to persons who were judged to be unclean, or at least unbaptized, but this image might not always have applied to the "house dogs" found in this context. Jewish sources include some references (from the centuries immediately following the time of Jesus) to "infidel dogs," "Gentile dogs," and even "Christian dogs." Christians, not surprisingly, sometimes returned the compliment, as in Philippians 3:2-4a.

Woman — The term here is *gunai*, the same word addressed to Mary in John 2:4 and Mary Magdalene in John 20:13 and 15. Both here and in John the term is not particularly respectful, and is regarded as at least mildly derogatory.

Let it be done for you — This translates a third person imperative, a grammatical construction not available in English. Perhaps the best way to understand this statement is to think of it as being in the same vein as the typical command of Captain Picard of the Starship Enterprise — "Make it so." This is what Jesus is saying here, but in a way that can only be phrased quite clumsily in English.

her daughter was healed — The word order in Greek is actually *healed the daughter of her from that hour was*. The point in the original text is to emphasize the healing action over any other possibility.

instantly — The phrase used is actually *from that hour*. In an era when precise time was largely a figment of someone's imagination, this phrase served as an equivalent to the modern concept expressed in the NRSV translation — *instantly*.

Parallels

Matthew uses the text of Mark 7:24-30 quite freely as a basis for this episode. While the length of the two accounts remains roughly the same, the details are changed significantly from the Marcan original to this account. As a simple example, Mark calls her a Phoenician woman of Syria (hence, the common translation of "a Syrophoenician woman"). Matthew calls her a Canaanite, a term which no longer has a contemporary referent, unless he uses it in a demeaning sense.

In Mark 7:24, Jesus enters a house, seemingly to avoid the crowds following him, but his efforts are futile and it turns out that he can't be hidden. This detail is not mentioned in Matthew, perhaps in an effort to maintain Jesus' "cleanliness," as merely entering the house of a Gentile could be taken as rendering him unclean.

169

Matthew's report of Jesus' effort to ignore the woman and her request (or demand), and the disciples' begging that he send her away are not found in Mark. Thus, these events are likely quite significant for Matthew. This image of Jesus is of someone who has been pursued by the crowds rather consistently and is seeking a refuge to rest for a brief time. As he moves in an area somewhat distant from his normal haunts, looking for some relief, a woman appears and demands a healing. At first Jesus resists both his disciples' urgings and the woman's demands, but eventually, after he interacts with her, the woman's humor, and her absolute conviction that Jesus can cure her daughter, impress him and he does what she has been asking for.

Matthew 8:13 records the only other cure of a Gentile (the Centurion's son in Capernaum) in the gospels. In both that episode and in the current story, the healing word is spoken at a distance and the cure is effected instantaneously. Again, it seems that this occurs to protect Jesus' ritual cleanliness by avoiding the need for him to actually enter a Gentile dwelling.

The People

As Individuals

One of the more unusual figures found in the stories of Jesus interacting with people in the gospels is the Canaanite woman found in this story. Not only is she a woman and a Gentile, she also displays a quick wit and a sense of humor even as she is consumed by the problems which are consuming her daughter. In a time when women were generally regarded rather doubtfully (as in John 4:27), this woman was not particularly bound by social conventions in her search for a cure for her daughter. Above everything else, she was persistent.

Clearly she was not Jewish, but she does use Jewish terms to address Jesus. Perhaps this desperate woman, hearing of a healer, sought out people who might help her approach him and seek a cure. It is certainly possible that the woman began by mouthing phrases she had been instructed in, not knowing what they actually

170

meant, in an effort to ensure the healer's help with her problem. It is as if she is seeking a magical cure for her daughter, one that the proper word will bring to pass, a word like *abracadabra*. It matters not that the healer happens to be Jewish while she is prostrating herself and subjecting herself to a representative of a race her ancestors (and likely her relatives), all regarded as contemptible at best.

What matters to this woman is the bright prospect of saving her daughter from the possession of the demon that is afflicting her. This is an attitude most parents can readily understand, certainly if their children have ever been afflicted by a problem which threatened their lives.

Even more, the woman is able to maintain a quick wit and sense of humor even in the face of being ignored by Jesus. When the disciples urged him to do what she wanted so she would go away, she must have felt as if she would have her miracle. To make things worse, the disciples' pleas were answered with Jesus' claim that he was not sent to help her. Her hope, which had been flickering and then brightening, must have flickered almost out.

In what can be understood as an act of desperation, she threw herself at his feet, likely impeding his progress, and simply begging for help. The answer came that the children's food shouldn't be thrown to the dogs. Rather than taking offense at being called a dog, even a house dog, she gave a response which showed both her quick wit and her acceptance of the probably humorous tone of Jesus' remark. Even dogs get the crumbs.

Even in asking for something that was the most important thing in her life at that moment, the woman was able to recognize that her needs were not necessarily the most important things in the world to anyone but herself. Rather than taking offense, rather than offering a stinging rebuke at this callous response to her request, the woman pointed out the weakness in the image used by Jesus.

Many people have the experience of having something said to them and then realizing exactly what they should have said in response a few hours, or days later. The woman had the much rarer experience of having something said to her and making the perfect response immediately.

171

And, taking her response as a sign of her deep faith, a faith so deep she was willing to view things realistically and acknowledge that she was in the wrong, asking for a terrible imposition from this healer, and knowing that what was so important to her was so inconsequential to him, Jesus did what she asked.

The picture of Jesus in this episode is certainly not what we might expect. Two weeks before this, Jesus tries to withdraw for a well-earned rest, but when the crowds follow him, he heals them and feeds them. Last week, when the disciples were faced with a storm that terrified them, he walks out on the surface of the lake and stills the storm. Now, when a woman appears asking for help for her daughter, Jesus begins by ignoring her, then he is rude to her, and only after she provides an impressive answer does he admit to being awed by her faith, and grants her demand.

This is hardly the caring and compassionate Jesus we expect to find in the gospels. He behaves in ways which would earn a rebuke from most parents to children who acted so rudely even to people they met even without knowing who the people were. Jesus is portrayed as a cold, rude, and quite ungenerous person. He refuses to even recognize the woman, then he refuses her request quite rudely, and only then, after a great response to his boorish behavior, does he grant her request.

As Images And Signs

The term used by Jesus, "children's food," can help us understand some of the images in this lesson. "Children" is often used as a sort of shorthand way of referring to the "children of Israel." The use of this phrase strengthens the image of Jesus' understanding of his ministry as directed to the Jews, as he states in Matthew 15:24.

The literal meaning of the term, "children's bread" can also be understood as a further reference to the eucharist and a comment on giving it to those who were not already part of the church. The eucharistic imagery was introduced with the feeding of the 5,000, and the mention of bread here can be taken as an echo of that mention. The story in general seems to function as a comment on the relationship which should exist between the Jewish core of the

Matthean church and the Gentile converts who were beginning to join it in ever greater numbers.

Matthew emphasizes that the ministry of Jesus is aimed at the Jews, who will then spread the word to the rest of the world. This is the same general pattern which is projected at the beginning of Acts. Unfortunately for the idea of a nice, neat pattern, things didn't work out quite the way they were expected to. The Day Of Pentecost was an event which centered on the Jewish population in Jerusalem, but Paul (and to a lesser extent Peter) soon found themselves involved with Gentile converts to the Christian ideas they proclaimed. The precise relationship was one which was not easily worked out, as the book of Acts makes clear.

The woman's comment about crumbs that fall from the master's table is an implicit recognition of the Jews as the masters (superiors) of Gentiles, particularly the people she comes from. While this certainly helped the Jewish Christians to feel better about the situation, not all Gentile converts were as willing to assume positions of subservience to the Jewish converts. This conflict would work itself out eventually, and largely as the number of Gentile Christians began to outnumber the Jewish Christians by substantial multipliers. Local situations could still present problems, however.

Further, Jesus ended up complimenting the woman on her great faith. This could certainly be interpreted as a comment against Jewish Christians, especially as most Jews didn't accept the Christian faith. Even a story that had many things which would make them happy ends on a note that was likely to cause problems for their self-image.

The disciples, in their suggestion to Jesus that he should do what the woman wants, basically that Jesus should do something, anything, just make her go away, are also familiar figures. It is often easier to take the simple route, just to make the problem go away. Don't really confront the issue, simply make it go away, get everybody to be quiet about these things, and eventually there will be no further problem. The disciples are certainly a reminder of the attitudes often seen when a problem rears its ugly attitude in the church.

The Action

In The Story

Underlying all the action of this story is the quest Jesus began in the lesson two weeks ago. He is still trying to find a little time for rest and contemplation, a quest which is still somewhat unfulfilled. In Mark, the action of the story is quite frenetic and the pace doesn't seem to let up from beginning to end. In Matthew, things are a little slower paced, but the search for a place for a retreat is still somewhat tedious and difficult to fulfill.

One aspect of the story which is somewhat out of character and a little unsatisfying is the attitude Jesus expressed toward the woman. First, he ignored her completely. When he had crossed the Sea of Galilee to escape the crowds, and they followed him anyway, he had compassion on them and healed the sick, then fed them (Matthew 14:13-21). The difference here seems to be that the crowds were Jewish and the woman was Canaanite.

It is difficult today to present derogatory terms from the first century with the same force they had at that time and place. Calling someone a Canaanite or a dog is simply not often offensive today. Different people use different ways to express the disdain inherent in such terms. In the *Cotton Patch* volumes, Clarence Jordan often replaced pejorative terms such as "Samaritan" with the terms "black" or "nigger." The replacement word is still quite offensive, even half a century after the use was first brought in. In this episode the woman is presented as black and Jesus said he was sent only to "needy white folks." Even today, many long years after the *Cotton Patch* versions were prepared, the tensions inherent in these terms still have a lot of validity, and more meaning in a modern context than the term "Canaanite."

It seems quite probable that the woman was a member of a group that the Jews at that time looked down upon. On the surface, Jesus seems to share that prejudice. He didn't answer her at all. This is not what we expect from Jesus, ignoring someone in need. The only answer available to this difficult situation is that Matthew seems to have allowed the theological understanding of the way in which the church was supposed to grow to shape his account of this incident.

In The Hearers

When first hearing this story, it is probable that the listeners heard it as a direct challenge to the exclusive nature of the Christian "club" to which they belonged. We know, from Acts, that there was a strong group of believers in the early church who held the view that a Christian had to become a convert to Judaism before they could become a Christian. It has long been understood that the audience for Matthew's Gospel included many former Jews who had embraced the Christian faith.

Into this group, which was seemingly quite proud of both their Jewish background and their Christian faith, Matthew casts this story of a woman from a background assumed to be unlikely to produce anyone even capable of faith, much less someone who was actually possessed by a faith strong enough to impress Jesus and gain the healing she sought for her daughter. The delay in the story between initial request and granting of the healing parallels the time between Jesus' ministry and the admission of Gentiles directly into the church.

The Sermon

Illustrations

If the preacher decides to include the optional portion of the lesson (Matthew 15:10-20) on this day, here is a story about the point:

A missionary in Africa once had a limited supply of printed resources to share with a growing number of believers. To make things go farther, he tore up some of the most bedraggled materials and distributed the resulting scripture portions to all who requested them, including a young boy.

A few days after giving the boy a portion of a gospel, the boy returned to the missionary in tears. The missionary asked what the problem was, and the boy said, "My dog is ruined."

"What happened?"

"My dog was the bravest hunter in the village. He would chase anything, even a lion. But, when I took the pages you gave me about the Prince of Peace, my dog ate some of them in the night. Now he is ruined, for he will never be fierce again."

There is some old doggerel about exclusive attitudes:
When you get to heaven, you will likely view
    Many folks whose presence will be a shock to you.
But keep it quiet, do not even stare,
    Doubtless there'll be many folks surprised to see you there!

Concerns about the sort of folks who are allowed to participate in the church, and their depth of faith, bring this to mind:

A gentleman once appeared at the church and asked to join. He was asked about the reasons why he wanted to join and he said, "Well, it was like this. Last night I was sleeping, and I woke up and heard a bug scratching on the pillow. But when I turned on the light and looked, I couldn't find any bugs. So I figure that was the Lord's way of telling me I should join the church."

There was some consternation among those who heard the story, and many doubts were expressed until one old deacon spoke up, "I move we take him in. We already have lots of members who have never even heard a bug scratch."

There are sometimes difficulties in dealing with the opportunities with which we are faced.

The sailors of Francis Drake, it is said, used to sit on the rocky coasts of England telling the boys of the countryside not about the pleasures of the sea, but the dangers. They spoke of high waves, stout winds, and gallant ships riding out the storms. They talked about such things until the country boys listening wanted it so much they ran away from home to be a part of Drake's expeditions.

There are times when it might be better if people really did ignore you.

A prisoner once dug a tunnel to escape from his captivity. When he escaped, he emerged in a school playground. As he emerged into the open air, he was so overjoyed that he shouted at a young girl standing nearby, "I'm free, I'm free."

"That's nothing," she said scornfully. "I'm four."

Approaches To Preaching

There is a danger in labeling things unclean, or identifying them as outside our area of responsibility. This lesson speaks powerfully against exclusivism and self-satisfaction in the church. Most particularly, separating one's self from what is unclean causes problems when what is unclean is actually a better witness to faith in Christ than that which is kept apart to maintain purity. Purity can become sterile.

Consider the contrast between the Canaanite woman, from a background of prejudice against the Jews with an immense faith in Jesus; and the population of Jerusalem, which will be clamoring for Jesus' death in a few weeks.

What defiles? This is the question of the optional portion of the Gospel Lesson appointed for this day. The lesson here is, in many ways, an answer to the question. Clearly what is important is faith, not some ritual cleanliness or list of qualifications.

The woman demanded a miracle, and wasn't prepared to leave until she got what she wanted. Are we sometimes too meek in our prayer? Do we sometimes hold back from challenging ourselves as we seek to serve God?

The early church was very willing to compete in the intellectual marketplace. Justin Martyr, for example, in the second century earned his living as a catechist, without any compensation from the church, only from the fees his students paid. Modern Christians often tend to shirk the call to witness to their faith. Not Christians alone, but also other religious traditions (for example, both

Islam and Hindu) try to legislate obedience to religious rules of conduct. It can be as if the rules won't stand on their own, but must be enforced by some sort of purity police.

The woman was very persistent in her prayers to Jesus to help her daughter. She met his objection with humor, but also restated her request. Persistent and insistent. It can seem as if both our prayers and our presence are being ignored just as thoroughly as were those of the Canaanite woman. It is important to realize this is not a new sensation, as it also appears in Psalm 28:1.

Once again, at least in the mention of bread (food), a eucharistic theme is present in this lesson. The crumbs can also be taken as a reference to the leftovers from the feeding miracle of two weeks ago. Twelve baskets of food that Jewish folks had no use for are now available for distribution to Gentiles.

www.ingramcontent.com/pod-product-compliance
Lightning Source LLC
Chambersburg PA
CBHW072051080426
42733CB00010B/2081